A WORD IN SEASON

A WORD
IN SEASON

Stuart Jackman

A LION BOOK

The articles in this book have previously appeared
in the magazines *Woman and Home*, *Woman's Realm*
and *My Weekly*.

Published by
Lion Publishing plc
Sandy Lane West, Oxford, England
ISBN 0 7459 3354 8
Albatross Books Pty Ltd
PO Box 320, Sutherland, NSW 2232, Australia
ISBN 0 7324 1316 8

First edition 1995
10 9 8 7 6 5 4 3 2 1 0

A catalogue record for this book is available
from the British Library

Printed and bound in Great Britain
by Biddles Ltd, Guildford and Kings Lynn

For Sheena,
constant companion on the journey
and for Nick, Morag, Max and Andrew,
who have joined us on the way.

Contents

Introduction   11

Christmas Stocking
More Than We Deserve   15
The Innkeeper's Wife   21
Songs of Love and Freedom   29
According to Luke   35
Merry Christmas Peter Brown   41
The Magic Men   47

Day By Day
Day By Day   57
A Great Past In Front Of Me   61
A Friend Indeed   65
Romance Has Many Faces   71
Tuppence Coloured   81
Beware of Experts   87
Brownie Points   93
Hidden Power   99
Africa Sings   103
A Question of Trust   109
Is Anyone There?   115
Blithe Spirits   121

Easter Eggs

Honest Doubt   129

New Every Morning   135

Easter Journey   141

The True Glory   147

Full Circle

All You Need Is Love   157

Let There Be Heroes   167

A Bouquet Of Brides   171

A Lovesome Thing?   177

Terms Of Reference   183

A Certain Style   187

The Gift Of Speech   193

Coming Through The Rye   199

A Traveller's Tale   213

The Year's at the Door   217

To make an apt answer is a joy to a man,
and a word in season, how good it is.

Introduction

He was waiting for me when I came out of the village Post Office; a short, square-rigged Commander RN (rtd) who read *The Times* over breakfast every morning, the lesson in the parish church on Sundays and the Riot Act to boisterous schoolboys unwise enough to skateboard on the pavement outside his house.

'Now then, Padre,' he said, brisk as an off-shore breeze. 'The word is you're retiring.' His ensign-blue eyes met mine accusingly as if I had boarded his ship without saluting the quarterdeck. 'True, is it?'

I nodded. 'End of this month.'

'So soon?' He shook his head. 'Sorry to hear that. Very sorry. You haven't done a bad job here. For a Nonconformist.'

I smiled. A dyed-in-the-wool Anglican, he had never forgiven us for executing Charles I and rejecting the Book of Common Prayer. 'Good of you to say so, Commander.'

He shrugged. 'Praise where praise is due.' He tilted his head, hands in the pockets of his blazer, thumbs protruding naval fashion. 'So, it's away on the tide, then. Off into the blue and a new landfall waiting over the horizon, eh?'

'Not exactly new. We're...'

But he was well into his boyhood-of-Raleigh routine now, immune to interruptions. 'You've picked the right season to go adventuring. Spring of the year. Clear skies and a friendly sea. Discoveries to be made. New friends, new scenes. Nothing to touch it.'

'Actually, we're retracing our steps,' I said, hating to disappoint him. 'Going back to Devon.' Where we had begun our married life forty years ago.

'Going back?' He frowned fiercely. 'That's a mistake

you'll live to regret. You can't go back, Padre. None of us can.'

'The prodigal son did,' I said gently. 'And was welcomed back with open arms.'

He gave me an affronted stare, embarrassed to be talking religion in the street on a weekday. And with a chapel man. 'I daresay, Padre. But that's different. I mean, he's scarcely a representative figure, is he?'

But that is exactly what he is. For we are all on a journey back to God from whom we come. Travellers on the Circle Line of life where birth and death are opposite platforms in the same station and home is at the top of the escalator in the sunlit splendour of the Kingdom where there is no yesterday and no tomorrow—only the eternal, ever-present Now.

It is my pleasure in this book to introduce some of my fellow travellers on that journey. Men and women with whom I have been privileged to share those gifts of God— love and laughter, courage and hope and a sense of wonder—which are the common speech of life as we know and live it day by day. People who, like the Commander, would be ashamed to be called images of God. Yet that is what they are—what we all are. Blurred images, perhaps, seen as through a glass darkly. But true images nonetheless, echoes of his Word, touched by his glory, honoured by his grace. For of such is the Kingdom.

Christmas
Stocking

MORE THAN WE DESERVE

We used to hang four stockings by the fire on Christmas Eve. One for Brooke, one for Morag and a last minute one for Hew who had not been expected until the New Year but got himself posted early for Christmas and arrived on December 22nd. The fourth was for Drew who had come as a bit of a surprise the year after we sold the cot.

They are all grown up now and long away, but one stocking remains, hanging in my mind bulging with memories. Every year, in the last magic hour before midnight, when the world holds its breath and waits for its Creator, I open that stocking and remember...

It is ten days before Christmas, 1955, and we have just

moved into the manse in Surrey, newly returned from five years on the other side of the equator. It is snowing steadily. This pleases Brooke and Morag (both very young) more than us because we have only one carpet—in the sitting-room. The few small rugs which had looked so chic on our polished wooden floors in Africa are not very welcoming to the feet on a cold winter's morning in England. We haven't much money, either. Enough, perhaps, to see us through an ordinary month until the first pay cheque arrives but nothing like enough for a month which includes Christmas.

I am in my study (frost on the windows, cold lino on the floor) doing melancholy sums when the doorbell rings. The man on the step says, 'Hullo, I'm Father Christmas.'

He doesn't exactly look the part. He wears a shabby overcoat and a black beret. He's in his fifties, myopic behind thick-lensed glasses, his tie frayed, a hole in one woollen mitten. I take him into the study, bracing myself for a hard luck story, miserably aware I have nothing to give him. 'Settling in?' he says cheerfully.

'More or less.'

He looks at the uncarpeted floor. 'Hard times?'

'A bit stringent, yes.'

He nods briskly. He has the blunt, weathered face of a street-market trader with thick-fingered hands to match, and his hair is sparse and grey. Yet there is something about him—an unexpected dignity, a kind of quiet alertness—which gives him stature and commands respect. Hugely magnified by those bottle glasses, his eyes hold mine, shrewd with understanding. 'Know the feeling, old son,' he says. 'Had my share of life's rough edges.' He sits down at my desk, pulls out his cheque book and a gold-capped pen and begins to write. 'I'm one of your congregation by the way.'

'Ah,' I am still very much the new boy in town trying to put names to the faces of some three hundred strangers on Sunday morning.

'Come up in the world now, mind.'

I nod politely. Through the window above his head I can see a big, black Mercedes standing outside the gate, contrasting oddly with his jumble sale clothes. 'Nice car. '

'Tax deductible,' he says. And grins. 'Unlike the suit I wear to church.'

He stands up and gives me a cheque. 'This is for you and yours, Minister. Merry Christmas.' And he is out through the door and away up the path to his car before I have finished stammering my thanks.

I look at the cheque in disbelief. Fifty pounds. And that was money in 1955.

Discreet enquiries subsequently showed him to be a wealthy, highly eccentric man with a string of small, back-street shops across south London and a house on the Downs bought for cash from a titled gentleman (who could no longer afford to keep it up). None of which detracted in the least from the generosity of his gift.

Hew arrived a week later, weighing in at just under nine pounds. We had a marvellous Christmas…

Half-past five on Christmas morning, 1944, and still black dark on the veranda of the military hospital outside Cairo. I waken under a pile of blankets (Egyptian winter nights can be cold), vaguely aware of a shadowy figure at the foot of my bed.

'Who's that?' I say sharply.

'Keep it down, mate,' a voice whispers hoarsely. 'It's only Father Christmas innit.' He drops something on the bed. 'Merry Christmas, me old china. Back 'ome in Blighty next year, eh?'

'Roll on the boat,' I say drowsily, convinced I'm dreaming, and drift back to sleep again.

But it is no dream. When the sun wakens me an hour later, all down the veranda (and in the ward behind us) men are sitting up in bed opening small, cotton bags. Inside are chocolate, cigarettes, matches, soap, a packet of razor blades, a big Jaffa orange and a pair of knitted socks. So it really was Father Christmas, heavily disguised as the ward orderly.

We grin at each other, as surprised and excited as if we were children again. There is much chatter and laughter as we swap socks to find the right size and trade chocolate for cigarettes with the non-smokers.

The ward sister arrives to take temperatures, keeping a watchful eye on Bombadier Willis who tends to nip into the ablutions before she gets to him and fill his mouth with hot water, thus ensuring another day in the comfort of a hospital bed. We show her our presents and she smiles, ignoring for once the untidiness of our bedclothes. 'No more than you deserve, boys,' she says with unusual gentleness. 'Courage doesn't go unnoticed, y'know.'

But we are not heroes wounded in action, bandaged and splinted. We are only the victims of the jaundice epidemic which filled the military hospitals in the Middle East that winter, unglamorously hollow-eyed and yellow.

When someone says as much, she shrugs. 'It's Christmas, isn't it? And Christmas is for everybody.' She grins. 'Even malingerers pretending to be Japanese spies.' And winks at Bombadier Willis. Who has the grace to blush.

She was right, of course. Christmas is for everybody, deserving or not...

Memories trigger other memories and now it's Christmas 1928, and my father and I are walking bravely through the Manchester sleet to see Father Christmas in one of the big shops in Market Street. Paulden's, I think it was.

Curiously enough, he is holding court in an underwater grotto in the basement. I don't know why and I don't ask. When you are five such questions are irrelevant. We go up to the top floor and enter a lift marvellously disguised as a submarine. Portholes (in a submarine?) through which paper fish peer at us cheerily, a compass, a big cardboard tube for a periscope. I find it totally convincing right down to the smell of wet clothes.

The lift attendant pulls a lever and down we go at breath-taking speed. He rolls one eye in mock terror (he is dressed as a pirate with a black patch over the other eye), slows the lift down and says, 'Fifty fathoms, me hearties.'

We step out onto sand. There is a real (stuffed) shark suspended threateningly on wires, deliciously scary. We walk past canvas rocks, a small wreck, fronds of crepe paper seaweed, a rusty anchor. And in the grotto, bearded, smiling and miraculously dry, Father Christmas himself sitting beside a small pile of presents (half-crown tickets) and a much larger one (shilling tickets).

He takes me on his knee hospitably. He has big knees and jolly eyes and smells agreeably of peppermint. I trust him implicitly.

My father stands rather stiffly in the entrance to the grotto, incongruous in his city suit and bowler hat, beside a life-size painting of a mermaid reclining in an enormous shell, her long, golden hair discreetly arranged.

Father Christmas asks me what I would like for Christmas (a politely worded question now, alas, replaced by the mercenary: 'What do you want?'). I tell him shyly. He exchanges glances with my father and nods. 'Well, son,' he says, 'I think I might manage that. The thing is, though, have you been a good boy?'

An expected question, much favoured by adults in those days. But before I can answer (needing time to think), my father says sharply, 'What on earth has that to do with it?'

Father Christmas's jaw drops. 'Pardon?'

'Christmas isn't a reward for being good,' my father says. 'The whole point is that we don't deserve it, can never deserve it. But God gives us his Son just the same. A gift, that's what Christmas is. Not a prize to be won, a gift to be accepted.' He looks meaningfully at the piles of presents and the half-crown ticket clutched in my hand. 'A *free* gift,' he says with enormous emphasis...

I smile now, my stocking of memories opened. Christmas has many faces. A shabby stranger with a cheque book, a ward orderly playing Santa Claus, a ham actor in a fake grotto. Part of its magic is that it is unexpected, as was the Child born in a manger of humble parents. Yet it is always the same face. The face of hope and wonder. The face of love.

My father was right, though. We don't deserve it. Thank God we don't have to.

THE INNKEEPER'S WIFE

(Statement made by Mrs Ruth Isaacs, wife of
Reuben Isaacs, landlord of The Royal David
Hotel, Bethlehem)

'Let's be clear about one thing, shall we? We didn't charge them. Not one penny. Not for their supper, nor the hot water and towels they needed later on, nor the milk and eggs for breakfast next morning.

'I'm not making excuses, mind. Maybe we did make a mistake—a big mistake. If we did, well that's something we've got to live with for the rest of our lives, Reuben and me. But at least we didn't take their money. 'On the house if not in the house,' as my husband said.

'Yes, well it's easy to be wise after the event. Looking back now, I wish we'd done better for them, even if it had meant us giving up our own room to them. And that's what it would've meant, you know. Oh, yes. We really were full that night. People sleeping all over the place—in the corridor, on the benches in the bar—anywhere we could get a mattress down. Glad to do it, too, they were, and pay over the odds for it. So the stable seemed the only place to put them at the time. At least they had a bit of privacy there. Just as well as things turned out.

'Now wait a minute, Mister. It wasn't like that. We didn't organize the census, did we? It wasn't our fault the town was crammed with strangers. If you're looking for someone to blame, look for that little busybody of a civil servant in Rome. It was his idea to turn the country upside-down in the middle of winter, not ours. We didn't force people to travel miles and miles through the worst weather of the year just to put their names on an official form in the place where they'd been born. You go and talk to those hard-faced bureaucrats in the Foreign Office. They're the ones who were responsible, not us.

'Our responsibility to our guests? Oh, really. I don't need the likes of you to teach me my job, thank you very much. Making travellers welcome and comfortable's our first priority and we're good at it, although I say it as shouldn't. Value for money—that's what we aim to give. Always have done. You've only to look at the comments in our Visitors' Book to see that. But we are only human, you know. It was going on for midnight by the time that couple got here and we'd been up since five that morning, run off our feet the whole blessed day, we're neither of us afraid of hard work—well, you can't afford to be in this business. But enough's enough.

'It was like the whole world was trying to get in here. Wet through and bad-tempered, most of 'em, demanding hot baths, meals—even room service if you please. A nightmare, that's what it was. A real nightmare. Like I said, I'm not making excuses, but when those two turned up in the middle of the night it was the last straw.

'Their names? No, we never did get their names. Not properly, anyway. Well, I mean, you can't very well ask someone to sign the book when you're putting them in the stable, can you? He called her Mary and she called him Joe and that was about as far as we got with names.

'They were working-class, of course, but quite respectable. What you'd call a decent young couple. At least, she was young. Just a girl, really. Didn't look old enough to be married, let alone expecting. But he was a good bit older and very protective. One of those big, quiet men, y'know? At his wits' end, poor fellow. They'd come all the way down from Nazareth in the north. Three days on the road, he said. And the weather was dreadful. They looked even more done in than we were and that's saying something.

'Sorry for them? Well, of course we were, she being the way she was and all. If there's one thing you don't need when you're carrying and near your time it's a three-day slog through the mud and the rain.

'She stood beside him in the doorway, white as a ghost, swaying on her feet, her eyes like two holes burned in a blanket. It nearly broke my heart to see her like that. There was something about her, you see—a sort of innocence, of wonder. Like a child with a secret. I remember how she looked at me, her eyes pleading, trusting. Believing we would help her.

'That's right, the stable. It was all we had to offer and... Oh, I see. That's it, is it? You've been listening to those smug, self-satisfied snobs with the big houses at the top of the town, have you? Wealthy folk with rooms to spare, who were tucked up in bed at the time and wouldn't have lifted a finger to help, even if they'd known. To hear them talk you'd think we'd put the young mother-to-be in some ramshackle old shed knee-deep in muck and open to the weather. Trust them to make a bad job worse. Typical.

'Well, let me tell you, it wasn't like that. It's a good stable. A cave, really, cut deep into the hillside behind the house. Dry as a bone and sheltered from the wind. Reuben got a fire going and brought in clean, fresh straw. And we gave them a lantern and blankets and made it all snug and warm. I took in hot soup and there was bread and cheese and a bottle of wine. I'm not saying it was ideal because it wasn't. But neither was it anything like as bad as people are saying. And, like I said, we didn't charge them for anything. A lot of people would've done but we didn't.

'Yes, I daresay. But we had no idea who they were, had we? Nobody had, not that night. The next morning, of course, it was quite a different story. That's if you believe the shepherds, anyway.

'It was all over by the time they showed up. Four o'clock in the morning and the baby safely born and sleeping in the manger. I'd just got the mother settled comfortably and tidied up a bit when the shepherds burst in, shouting and singing, wild with excitement or drink—I didn't know which. We usually leave a couple of jars of wine for them on a winter's night. It can be bitter cold up on those hill fields with the sheep and they come down in twos and threes—take turns, like—for a warm and a wet. I thought that was what they'd been doing.

'Angry? I was horrified. I mean, the last thing a woman wants in those circumstances is a bunch of drunken louts gawping at her. Great, hulking oafs stinking of garlic and sheep, babbling some crazy story about a light in the sky and the sound of angels singing and a voice telling them the baby born in our stable was—well, God.

'That's right. God. Oh, I really set about them then, believe me. I don't often lose my temper but I lost it then and no mistake, shouting at them to shut up and get out. I was frightened, you see. Angry and frightened. It was being so tired, I suppose. I was aching all over and my nerves were stretched tight and I was past caring what I said or did, I just wanted to be rid of them and their silly, blasphemous talk. But they seemed not to hear me, as if I wasn't there. They dropped to their knees, not looking at me, staring at the tiny baby in the manger.

'The noise had wakened him, as well it might, but he wasn't frightened. Just lying there with his eyes wide open. Marvellous eyes, he had. Blue, like all new-born babies, and shining. Filling his little face like two brilliant stars.

'He looked straight at me as if he knew who I was and— well, everything about me. As if I was the child and he already a man. And all the anger drained out of me and I felt myself falling and would've gone down if Reuben hadn't caught me. I closed my eyes and felt his arms around me.

' "Oh, Reuben," I said, choking over the words. "What have we done? What have we done?" I must've fainted then, because the next thing I knew I was sitting propped up against the wall of the cave and the shepherds had gone and the baby was sleeping again.

'I looked at his mother and she smiled, her face radiant. "Poor dear," she said. "You must be worn out."

'I felt the prickle of tears in my eyes. Healing tears, if you know what I mean. Tears of shame and relief. "I'm sorry," I whispered. "So very sorry."

'She shook her head. "There's no need to be. You've already done so much for us—for him."

' "But not enough," I said, remembering those searching eyes. "Not near enough."

' "You've helped my son into the world," she said. "And it won't be forgotten."

'Do I believe? That he was God, you mean? I don't know, I honestly don't know. He'll be five now, if he's still alive. They disappeared, you know. Some of our guests left the next morning—complaining about the noise in the night—and we put the little family in a decent room and told them they could stay as long as they liked—no charge.

But a couple of days later, when I went up to call them to breakfast, they'd gone. Taken the child and—well, just vanished. Went across the desert to Egypt—or so people said. Just in time, too. The soldiers came the next day.

'It's hard to imagine God—the God who made heaven and earth—growing up as a schoolboy. Playing with his friends in the street, running errands for his mother, grazing his knees, needing to be comforted. It's not the sort of thing you associate with God, is it? I mean, imagine being a teacher and having God in your class, asking questions you can't answer, knowing more than you'll ever know. How could that be?

'Looking back, it all seems like a dream. Too wonderful—and scary—to be true. Most of the time I don't think about it. Tell myself it never really happened. What else can I do? How would you feel if you believed the mother of God came knocking on your door on a winter's night, desperate for help and nowhere to go—and you put her in the stable to have her baby? How else can I live with that except by trying to forget it?

' "It won't be forgotten," she said. And she was right, you know. However hard I try, I can't forget it.

' "It's over," Reuben says to me sometimes. "Whatever the truth of it, it's over." But is it? Why would God get himself born as a baby unless he was going to grow up and become a man? A man to change the world?

' "We've heard the last of him," Reuben says.

'But have we?

'Sometimes, when things get on top of me and I can't sleep, I go to the kitchen and take a lantern up the hill to the stable, the way we did that night. And they're there to welcome me, Mary and her husband and her baby. I know it sounds foolish and perhaps it is. I expect I look pretty silly standing there in that empty cave talking to myself. But it does something for me no priest or church has ever been able to do.

'I see that little, innocent face with those wise, starry eyes and hear his mother's voice forgiving me. And all my worries disappear and I'm at peace with myself. I don't know how or why and it doesn't really matter. In my heart, beyond all reason or doubting, I know who he is.'

SONGS OF LOVE AND FREEDOM

T hey come every year in the week before Christmas; children singing carols on the doorstep. An echo, perhaps, of that eerily beautiful song which filled the night sky over Bethlehem so long ago. I like to think so.

Admittedly it's often a flawed echo. The singers have a limited repertoire (a couple of verses of 'Good King Wenceslas', a fragment of 'Silent Night') and their voices are enthusiastic rather than tuneful. But the thought is there. And once in a while a small miracle happens.

As it did for us last Christmas Eve when three young schoolgirls rang our doorbell and sang 'Love Came Down At Christmas' in close harmony and with a kind of transparent sincerity which brought a lump to my throat. We opened the door and saw them standing under the porch light, breath smoking in the frosty air, eyes like stars.

Sheena gave them some money and said, 'Any chance of an encore?'

They smiled shyly, nodded to each other and broke into 'I Saw Three Ships', jaunty as a sea shanty, bubbling with laughter. We both clapped. They blushed modestly, wished us a Merry Christmas and skipped away down the drive.

'Curious little carol,' Sheena said when they had gone.

'Yes.' Three ships sailing into a landlocked hill-village in Judea on Christmas Day in the morning. I wondered what the harassed innkeeper would have made of that? Another miracle after a night of miracles? I decided he would probably have taken it in his stride. When God has just been born in your stable, the sight of ships sailing merrily over fields and hedgerows would scarcely raise an eyebrow.

'Perhaps it means all our ships come in at Christmas,' Sheena said, eyeing the gaily-wrapped presents waiting under the tree.

I thought it a pleasant fancy and said so, but I had to wait until the summer to discover the truth within it...

On the last Saturday in June we were in Italy, heading south down Lake Como in the late afternoon aboard a little ship (well, all right, a boat). A day of sunlight and blue water, the light breeze scented with flowers. Behind us, the Alps towered snow-covered and massive. Ahead and on either side, lesser but still impressively high mountains rising steep out of the lake, heavily wooded on their lower slopes where the distant villages, bright with hydrangeas and scarlet geraniums, seemed to float on the water like extravagant Ascot hats. A majestic setting, tranquil, untouched by time. I remember thinking that if there had been a lake in Eden it would surely have looked like this.

From the foredeck of the boat we could see the windows of the monastery at Piona winking through the trees on the point, a small crowd waiting on the jetty. As we drew nearer we heard the sound of singing. Children's voices rising and falling like water in a fountain. They clustered on the jetty, twenty or so little figures, the girls in summer dresses with ribbons in their hair, the boys in white shirts and dark trousers. A band of pilgrims dressed in their best for a visit to the monastery, heads tilted back, faces shining with excitement. And the singing reaching out to us in welcome.

It was a moment of pure pleasure. A world away from those three young girls who had sung of love and little ships in the dark of an English winter, yet possessing the same heart-stopping beauty. The singing children in the mellow sunlight, the chuckle of water under the prow, the magnificent backdrop of silent, listening mountains. It was like a scene from an opera, needing only a Pavarotti to complete it. Although I doubt if even his glorious voice could have moved us quite so deeply as the artless integrity of that youthful little choir.

Shepherded by two smiling nuns, the children came on board still singing. Cherubic faces straight out of a Michelangelo painting, small hands clutching presents to take back home to Milan. Tiny baskets of flowers for Mamma, miniature bottles of the monks' herbal liqueurs for Papa.

'You like the singing, Signore?' The man sitting beside us was straight-backed with grey hair and an authentic Roman nose. Old soldier written all over him.

'E magnifico,' I said.

He smiled politely at my accent. Italians, unlike the French, are a forgiving people. 'You know what they sing?'

I shook my head. Folk songs, perhaps? The Italian equivalent of 'Cherry Ripe' or 'Strawberry Fair'?

'Freedom songs,' he said proudly. 'From the war, no? Songs of the partisans.'

I remembered this had been partisan country where the sturdily independent mountain men and women had harried the German rearguard as the Allies pushed up from the south. 'History now,' I said.

'Si. Long time ago. But we still remember the songs.'

'And teach them to your children?' Sheena said.

He nodded. 'Children need heroes, Signora, brave men who fought and died for our freedom. Is good we not forget.'

We were well out into the lake again now, Bellagio just visible far ahead at the tip of its peninsula, the shadows beginning to gather along the western shore. With the sudden tiredness of the very young, the children fell silent, curling up on the seats, their heads on each other's shoulders. I found myself thinking of another lake, another time. And of a young mother-to-be singing to the child moving within her. Mary of Nazareth, the mother of God.

He has shown strength with his arm
and scattered the proud in the imagination
  of their hearts;
He has put down the mighty from their seats
and exalted those of low degree...

Stirring stuff, revolutionary, triumphant. A freedom song for bugles and drums, the words taken (so the scholars tell us) from the song of the Jewish partisans two thousand years ago. Men of faith and courage dedicated to the overthrow of the Roman legions—the proud and the powerful—who held their land in thrall; fighting to prepare a way for Messiah, the long-promised King who would come to set his people free.

On Mary's lips it became the Magnificat—the first Christmas carol. A prophetic song for the advent of her Son, the true Messiah. Not the warlike King they all expected, ruling by force of arms. But a King born to rule in the power of love, sharing his people's suffering, giving hope to the oppressed, comfort to the poor, peace in the hearts of all who recognize him.

And suddenly, out there on the lake, it all came together in my mind. The carols on the doorstep, the singing on the jetty, the song that Mary sang. The truth of Christmas. Not a sentimental story, frail as a candle-flame in the winter wind, but a statement of fact like the blaze of the summer sun, strong, universal, timeless. As relevant today in our uneasy world as it was that night when the angels sang over Bethlehem. And as liberating.

All the way down to Bellagio I sat among those sleeping children and thought of the three ships which came sailing in on Christmas Day, bringing their cargo of peace and love and freedom.

The three gifts of Christmas.

ACCORDING TO LUKE

It was six o'clock in the evening, two days before Christmas, and I was a hundred miles from home, stranded in a small country town.

The mechanic said the trouble was the dynamo and did I live locally? I shook my head, knowing what was coming next. 'Only you'll need a new one,' he said, 'and I can't touch it tonight.'

He went on to say there was a decent little hotel in the square and if I came back about nine-thirty in the morning he would have the car ready for me. 'Best I can do, I'm afraid, sir.'

I booked a room for the night, rang my wife, ate a leisurely (and surprisingly good) meal and decided to go for a walk before turning in. It was a dry night but cold, the streets deserted. I walked past the lighted shop windows, down to the bridge over the river and back again without meeting anybody. There was a church in one corner of the square, the lantern in the porch inviting. On an impulse, I went up the steps and into the nave.

Inside, it was all shadows and stillness, just a single spotlight focus on the Crib beside a huge tree topped with a silver star. They had gone to a lot of trouble with the Crib; real straw on the floor of the open-sided stable, carved wooden figures of the shepherds and Wise Men, the inevitable donkey and a mild-eyed ox which was pure Disney. And Mary, of course, sitting protectively beside the manger with her husband standing behind her. All very traditional—if a little too cosy.

I sat down in the front pew, remembering all the Cribs of Christmas past, hearing the echo of children's voices singing carols, seeing again the half-forgotten faces of friends I had known. It was warm in the church and peaceful. My eyelids soon began to droop...

I was almost asleep when the light above the crib flickered and dimmed. Around me, the air was suddenly ice cold. I felt the hairs rise on the back of my neck as somebody settled in the pew beside me with an eerie, rustling sound like a bird coming to rest, or a ghost materializing out of the shadows.

'Charming little Crib.' The voice was cultured, easy; the voice of a man at home with words. As he spoke, the air grew warm again, the spotlight blazed at full strength with a vivid, unearthly brilliance. 'Not quite as I described it, perhaps. But beautifully done.'

Seized with excitement tinged with disbelief, I turned and saw a good-looking man in a dark blue cloak fastened with a silver clasp, sandals on his feet, hands folded comfortably in his lap. Clean, strong-fingered hands. Healer's hands. I knew who he was then; Luke, the physician turned author, oddly out of place in that English church. Out of time, too. Two thousand years out of time. But real. So real it was difficult to believe he existed only in my imagination.

'Mind you,' he said, 'Matthew wouldn't like those Wise Men.'

'He wouldn't?' I said cautiously, afraid he might disappear as abruptly as he had arrived.

He shook his head, his dark eyes amused. 'In his book, they were never anywhere near that stable. By the time they showed up, Joseph had found lodgings in a house in the town.'

'A small point,' I said forgivingly. I've always had a soft spot for Matthew, that cheerful, loyal little sparrow of a man.

'Not to Matthew, though.' He smiled the sort of confident smile a good doctor gives an anxious patient. 'A stickler for detail, our Matthew. All those years in the tax office, I suppose. I take it you've read his book?'

'Many times and with great pleasure.'

He nodded. 'Good solid writing with a punch in it. Pity about the first chapter, though—that long list of names tracing the Master's lineage right back to Abraham. Tedious and really quite unnecessary.' He sighed. 'Knowing where to begin is always difficult, even for professional writers and we were neither of us that. Once he got into his stride with that beautifully understated story of the Wise Men and Herod, he never looked back. But that opening chapter's very heavy going. Out of character, too. He wasn't a dull man, y'know. Anything but.'

'Your opening sets the scene brilliantly. I like it very much.' I recalled that astonishing encounter between Gabriel and Mary and the tie-in with the birth of John the Baptist. Just the right note of mystery, of something unprecedented waiting in the wings. The writing has a serene, dreamlike quality, ripe with promise. And then the mood changes abruptly. The census pin-pointing the date for us; the long trek down from Nazareth in the winter weather; the trauma of the cold, inhospitable stable. Weariness, the uncaring face of bureaucracy, anxiety, rejection. And, suddenly, the glory. The angel choir singing in the night sky. The shepherds running through the sleeping town. The beauty of the Child lying in the manger. 'I suppose it really was like that?' I said.

'Absolutely,' he said with a hint of asperity. 'I did take time to do my homework, y'know. My sources were impeccable.'

'I'm sure they were.'

'Most of what follows I borrowed from Peter. So did Matthew. I expect you've noticed that?'

I said that a great deal of my time in college had been spent comparing the four Gospel narratives.

'Yes?' he said, amused. 'Well, we switched the order of events around a little to point up the meaning, added a few human touches here and there, fleshed it out. But Peter gave us the bones of the story.' He smiled. 'He couldn't read, y'know. But like most illiterates, his memory was phenomenal. The whole three years of the Ministry were carried in his head—names, places, conversations—all on instant recall. Remarkable.'

'I know.' Peter, the big, impetuous fisherman from Galilee, tactless, outspoken, transparently honest, dictating his book to young John Mark and, with characteristic generosity, letting the boy sign it as his own. It is the shortest of the four Gospels and the most gripping—the words set down with a sharp, unpolished urgency as they had come tumbling out of his mouth. Only the broad Galilean accent is missing.

As if reading my thoughts, Luke said, 'He was in a hurry, you see; not getting any younger.' He grinned. 'No more diplomatic, either. And Nero's spies closing in on him. He was desperately anxious to get something down on paper before it was too late and the cross claimed him as it had claimed the Master. No time for Christmas or the early years in Nazareth. He was intent only to highlight the miracles, the teaching, the awesome personality of the man he recognized as the Son of God.'

'Is that why he began with the baptism in the Jordan?'

'Where else? For him it was the obvious starting point. The declaration of the Master's divinity. That voice from heaven like a thunderclap booming out over the crowd by the river: "You are my beloved Son." Magnificent.' He shrugged ruefully. 'My little tale of angels and shepherds seems slight in comparison, I'm afraid.'

'Not really,' I said. 'It's something we can all relate to. The miracle birth we've all experienced and wondered at. A beginning we can understand preparing us for the astonishing events to come. You've given us the real Christmas—the triumph of love over hatred and fear. We'll always be grateful to you for that.'

'Yes, well,' he said shyly, 'I thought it was important. The human angle, y'know. God trusting himself to us—a helpless infant in a largely uncaring world—in the hope that we would trust ourselves to him. Not as important as Easter, of course. That's the climax of the story. What it's really all about. The final triumph of the love that came down at Christmas.'

'Ah, yes,' I said. 'But there can be no resurrection without a death. And no death without a birth. We couldn't begin to celebrate Easter—let alone believe it—if we had no Christmas to celebrate first.'

He looked at me, his eyes approving. 'If you've grasped that, my friend, then I'm content. As Peter and Matthew will be.'

'And John?' I said quietly.

'Ah, John...' He sighed. 'Now there's a writer, if you like. He lifted the story into a new dimension, exploring depths we dared not plumb, scaling heights we dared not climb.

We told what happened, as well as we could. He told us why. A *tour de force* we couldn't begin to match. Beautifully crafted, amazingly perceptive. For him, the beginning and the end were one. The circle of eternity complete and whole.' He shook his head admiringly, 'That opening poem—the prologue to his book—is sheer perfection.'

In the beginning was the Word, and the Word was with God, and the Word was God. The immortal words rose up in my mind, majestic, universal, sonorous with meaning. Before time and through time and beyond time, building to that glorious climax: *And the Word was made flesh and dwelt among us, full of grace and truth.*

'Out of this world,' I said. 'The kingdom beyond all imagining.'

Luke nodded, his face transfigured, radiant with a shining which dimmed the spotlight. ' "No man has ever seen God," ' he quoted in a hushed voice. ' "The only Son, who is in the bosom of the Father, he has made him known." That says it all, my friend.'

I turned to look at the little figure in the manger, the effigy of the Child whose coming into the world changed the shape of history and made God our friend again. Saw him glowing in the darkness, rainbow-hued through the prism of tears—the Daystar bright around whom all life revolves, in whom all life finds its beginning and its destiny. And felt his peace fill my mind.

'Let me wish you a merry...' I turned back to Luke and stopped short. There was nobody there. I was alone in the pew.

'You and your imagination,' my wife said the next day when I told her.

And, of course, she was right. And yet...

MERRY CHRISTMAS
PETER BROWN

He was eight years old that Christmas and his name was Peter Brown. An English name and he could speak English (albeit with a South African accent you could hang your hat on) but he was much more fluent in Afrikaans. For Peter was a Cape Coloured; a child of mixed heritage, neither black African nor white European but a complex mix of the two. He was cheerfully polite, with smiling dark eyes in a face the colour of plain chocolate and a head of tight black curls. One of God's children cruelly disadvantaged in an unhappily divided country of immense wealth and grinding poverty.

It's almost forty years now since I last saw him but his face still haunts me. A kindly little ghost of Christmas past who comes into my mind late on Christmas Eve as I sit by the fire, look at the presents waiting under the tree and remember yet...

Christmas is a midsummer feast in the Transvaal and by 9.30 on Christmas morning the temperature was well up in the nineties in the little, iron-roofed church in the Coloured Location outside Pretoria. An arid, unlovely place in stark contrast to the tree-lined, flower-scented beauty of the white suburbs. Tumbledown shacks lining narrow, unpaved streets, standpipes for water, bucket sanitation, the smoke of cooking-fires. Yet the people there were decidedly colourful.

From the high pulpit I looked out over rows of crowded wooden benches at a kaleidoscope of colour. Gaudily printed dresses run up on ancient sewing machines, astonishing hats festooned with paper flowers, cotton gloves dyed bright pink, yellow, royal blue, crimson. And the excited, joyful faces ranging from almost pure black through a variety of shades of brown to freckled ivory. Plus a sprinkling of dark gold topped with straight, blue-black hair—the distinctive features of the Chinese/African cross.

We sang 'Once in Royal David's City' (made poignant by the fact that the congregation came from homes only a little less primitive than that lowly cattle shed), our voices drowning the shrill piping of the battered harmonium.

Earlier that morning I had sung the same carol with my white congregation in the chaste beauty of their modern church on one of Pretoria's fashionable avenues. No gaudily camouflaged poverty there; the clothes as elegantly expensive as the cars parked outside, the Christmas tree magnificently dressed, the flowers tastefully arranged. And on the communion table, the focus of every eye, the Crib, a masterpiece of African woodcarving. Small, bearded shepherds, richly robed Wise Men as portentous as the gifts they carried, Joseph quietly dignified, Mary serene, the tiny figure in the manger exquisitely made.

This was Christmas for the well-to-do white masters; artistic, deodorised, just a touch sentimental. A world away from that bleak stable and the rejection and danger of that humble birth in Bethlehem of which we sang so politely.

Here, in the dust and sweat of the Coloured shanty-town, we were much closer to the truth. No tree to stand tall beside the pulpit. A handful of flowers wilting in a cracked china vase. Worn floorboards, peeling paint, circling flies. But all this went unnoticed. The important thing was the Crib, a life-size, genuine wooden manger stuffed with real straw standing in pride of place below the pulpit. No miniature shepherds. No Wise Men. No little wooden donkey. But there was a baby, a plump, contented baby boy with the face of a sunburned angel. He was the newest addition to the congregation, born only four weeks ago and doing very nicely, thank you.

When a Coloured congregation sings it does so with tremendous enthusiasm, creating a great tidal wave of music which rolls down the church and up into the rafters, breaks on the iron roof and then swirls out through the open door. The volume of sound has to be heard to be believed—and even then takes some believing. The high keening of the women rises out of the men's deep groundswell (which makes the walls tremble), and the harmonies are too intricate to be written down. Impossible to resist it. All you can do is surrender yourself to it like a swimmer in a mill-race. Yet through it all, the baby in the manger slept undisturbed, the round, milk-chocolate face placidly innocent, the full lips parted, the tiny hands curled into fists.

'*Where a mother laid her baby in a manger for his bed...*' Suddenly the words were full of meaning, the mystery of that long-ago birth revealed as a living, breathing reality we could all see and touch and wonder at. I looked at the sleeping child, the swaying rows of eager, shining faces, and blinked back tears. So much poverty, so little to look forward to. Yet such happiness, such trust.

Services in a Coloured church are always uninhibited and sometimes surprising. Caught up in the rapture of worship, people do unexpected things. A slow, stately dance in the aisle expressing adoration. The unrehearsed (and therefore entirely convincing) acting of a parable by the children. A solo, perhaps, or a duet.

Jonas Johnson, the senior member of the church, his wrinkled face very black below his white hair, always sat in a chair beside the pulpit to keep me informed about what would happen next. So I was not entirely unprepared when, just before the sermon, he said in a penetrating whisper, 'Jannie Coetzee's going to sing a carol now, Reverend. For Peter Brown.'

I knew about Peter, of course. We all did, all of us in that congregation. He was sitting beside his mother on the front bench—as he had sat with her only ten days ago at his father's funeral. The police were still officially looking for the hit-and-run driver who had left Daniel Brown to die by the roadside. But nobody expected them to find him.

Alone among all the children in the church that Christmas morning, Peter was empty-handed. No favourite present to bring proudly to the service. No presents at all, in fact, and probably no Christmas dinner, with the funeral expenses to be met.

I smiled approvingly at Jonas. 'That's good.'

He nodded gravely.

Jannie came up the aisle to stand beside the Crib; in his early twenties, white teeth in a handsome face the colour of *café au lait*, tall and easy in a white shirt and black trousers. And a voice to melt your heart. The congregation settled expectantly as he began to sing unaccompanied.

It wasn't a carol in the accepted sense of the word. Not 'Silent Night' or 'While Shepherds Watched'. Not even 'White Christmas', an inexplicable favourite with those people who had never seen snow. He looked straight at Peter Brown and sang: 'The Little Boy that Santa Claus Forgot'. It was a slight, popular song of the day, sentimental to the point of being maudlin, about a small boy with no father to creep into his bedroom on Christmas Eve and fill his stocking. But sung to that silent, listening congregation, in a voice like black velvet, it was a gift to match those of the Magi. A little human story of hope and heartbreak to which every man, woman and child in the church could immediately relate; simply told, indescribably moving.

It's quite usual for a Coloured congregation to applaud after the sermon (and sometimes during it), or after a solo. But nobody applauded Jannie that morning. When he finished there was an electric silence in the church. The women sat with tears rolling down their faces. The children were solemn-eyed, the men tight-lipped. I stood up to thank him, saw Peter Brown's small, crumpled face and could find no words to speak.

And then a small boy halfway down the aisle stood up, clutching a large teddy bear. Not a new one. Probably handed down from some white family whose child had long outgrown it. One ear was missing and the head wobbled a bit, but it was clean and cuddly and obviously much loved by its new owner. He walked up to the front bench and put the teddy into Peter's arms. 'Merry Christmas, Pete,' he said shyly.

He was followed by a procession of children, each of them bringing a present. A wooden engine, several brightly-coloured picture-books, a scarf, a jigsaw puzzle— even a doll to keep the teddy company. They piled them on the bench beside him and gave some to his mother to hold for him. Peter sat round-eyed with astonished delight. His mother smiled through her tears.

And then the applause began. A thunderclap of sound, the church a forest of arms raised high above the heads, palms smacking together in unison, feet stamping on the wooden floor. And everyone laughing. Excited laughter, healing, restoring. And Peter, surrounded by the evidence of a Christmas beyond his dreams, his face one enormous grin.

When the clapping finally stopped, Jonas nodded to me. 'We'll have the sermon now, Reverend, please,' he said, his eyes twinkling. 'If you're ready.'

I don't remember a word I said in the sermon. Not that it mattered. The children had said it all for me, far more eloquently than I could have done, demonstrating the truth of the Christmas miracle; the winter of the spirit, shrouded in darkness and cold despair, suddenly warm and filled with light as they responded to God's gift of his Son by bringing gifts of their own to Peter Brown.

It was the baby in the Crib who rescued me that morning, waking up with a little gurgle of pleasure which cut into my halting, unnecessary words. I stopped in mid-sentence, looked at him and smiled. The congregation smiled back at me forgivingly. We sang one last carol, shared in the blessing and went to our homes in peace.

Had it all been secretly arranged beforehand? I don't think so. Miracles, however small, always come as a surprise. They are not arranged, they just happen. As one happened in the church that day, when God touched the hearts of his children and they responded in love.

Every child eventually realizes that Santa Claus is really his father—a miracle explained, if you like. But the miracle of Christmas, as Peter Brown discovered, is that our true Father is God who comes to make our dreams reality. A miracle like that, you can't begin to explain it. All you can do is believe it.

THE MAGIC MEN

I t all began with an early Christmas card from a friend
in New Zealand. He had chosen a traditional theme
featuring the Magi, those three Wise Men who
hitched their wagon to the Christmas star and came riding
out of the desert to frighten Herod with their story of a new
king born in Bethlehem.

But although the theme was traditional, the treatment
was modern. No flowing robes, no camels. Instead, the
Magi wore overcoats and gloves and carried suitcases. The
card showed them going through Customs at the airport
and obviously having trouble persuading the officers that
their gifts should be duty-free. A wry little comment on our
unchanging preoccupation with bureaucratic trivia in the
presence of momentous events.

I put it up on the mantelpiece, the first of many. It was

the last thing I saw before I switched off the light and went up to bed. Perhaps that's why I had the dream...

Fifteen minutes out of Basra, 28,000 feet up in the blue Arabian sky, stewardess Liz Parker walked into the forward galley of the big jet and pulled the curtain across the doorway. 'That man in D3,' she said, looking flustered, 'who is he exactly?'

Rawlins, the chief steward, picked up the passenger list. 'D3? That's the old boy who boarded in Karachi for Jerusalem, isn't it? Yes, here we are. Mr Melthazpar. Odd sort of name.'

'Odd sort of man, too,' Liz said. 'He keeps—well, changing. One minute he's a big, round-faced man with red hair and a weight problem. The next he's tall and thin, dark eyes, narrow face—like a professor or something.'

Rawlins grinned. 'I did warn you about those cocktails, love. What you've got is a classic...'

'What I've got,' Liz said sharply, 'is the shakes. Because sometimes he's a third man. Black hair, black beard, dressed like a bishop. And, just now and again, they're all there at the same time. Three separate men sitting in a row, arguing.'

Rawlins pulled the curtain aside and stood just outside the galley, looking casually down the length of the aircraft. 'Red hair and a complexion to match,' he said.

Liz nodded. 'That's how he looked when he boarded.'

'There you are then. Nothing to get excited about. He's...' Rawlins's smile froze. 'Hang about. Now he looks like one of those trendy clerics.'

'Black hair and beard?'

'Right.' Rawlins stepped back into the galley and checked the passenger list again. 'Melthazpar. Home address: Karachi. Ah. Wait a bit. He's put his occupation as magician.'

'On the stage, you mean?'

Rawlins nodded. 'That explains it. He's one of those illusionist chaps. Quick change artiste. Probably just running through his act.'

'In the third row of a 747?' Liz said incredulously.

Rawlins shrugged. 'So he's adaptable.'

The taxi driver pulled into the kerb outside the arrival terminal at Jerusalem's Atarot airport. The heavily-built man with red hair climbed into the back seat. 'The office of the President, if you please,' he said, his deep voice strongly accented.

The traffic, as always, was chaotic. Threading his way down Paratrooper Avenue, the driver heard voices behind him, glanced in the mirror and was startled to see three men on the rear seat. But when he drew up at Government House only one got out. Fat, red-haired, fumbling for his wallet. The other two had disappeared.

'Have you an appointment, sir?' the security guard asked. A formidable ex-sergeant-major, he stood foursquare in the vestibule, doing his job, barring the way.

The red-haired man produced a card, apparently out of thin air. 'Have this sent in to him. He'll see me.' Five minutes later he was seated opposite the President.

'A what?' the President said.

'A King,' Melthazpar said. 'Of the Jews.' He smiled. 'Just born.'

The President stared at him. And blinked. Melthazpar was now a scholar, thin-faced, tall, angular as a stick insect in his chair.

'A King?' The President licked his lips nervously. 'But that's impossible.'

The scholar inclined his head gravely and was at once a black-bearded priest. 'I think not, sir. It is said that with God all things are possible. And this one comes from God and will one day return to God.'

'Won't we all?' the President said, trying to smile.

'Indeed.' And now it was the scholar again. 'But not quite in the same way.'

The President closed his eyes for a moment and dug his fingers hard into his thigh under the desk. His doctors had warned him about this. Too many problems, too much stress. Middle East politics were a young man's game and he was no longer young, though younger than he looked. When he opened his eyes again he was relieved to see the man sitting opposite was big and heavy with astonishingly red hair.

'Are you all right, Mr President?' Melthazpar said.

The President nodded unhappily. He had a headache and his ulcer was playing up and his hands were suddenly very cold. 'Where is this—this King?'

'In Bethlehem.' The red-haired man was standing now, the scholar and priest beside him.

'We would like to go there now,' the priest said.

'With your permission, sir,' the scholar said.

'To give him our gifts,' the red-haired man said.

The President swallowed hard. 'Gifts?' He felt for the alarm button under his desk and failed to locate it.

'Gold,' the scholar said.

'Incense,' the priest said.

'Basil,' the red-haired man said. 'The kingly herb.' They looked at each other and nodded as if, for once, in full agreement. And were immediately one man, dressed in a clerical collar and priestly gown, black-bearded, dignified. His smile made the President shiver.

Melthazpar went in the President's car, driven by the President's chauffeur, tailed (though he didn't know this) by two Secret Service agents in a rather battered Fiat.

The six mile journey through the Jaffa Gate and out along the Beersheba road to David's little city on a hill took only a few minutes. The car stopped outside the hotel in the main square. The red-haired man got out and became three men, arguing bitterly, as they had done all the way from Karachi, about who should go in first to see the King.

At the reception desk the clerk was apologetic. There

wasn't a room to be had. 'It's the census, gentlemen,' he said. 'The town's bursting at the seams.'

The scholar said they weren't looking for rooms. Only for the King.

A slightly hunted look came into the clerk's eyes. He had had a busy day and was in no mood for jokes. 'King, sir?' he said guardedly.

'A royal child,' the priest said. 'Newly born.'

The clerk shook his head. 'The only baby we've got staying is the son of a working-class couple from the north. They're out in the garage round the back. There wasn't room for them in...'

'Garage?' the red-haired man said angrily. 'You've put the child in a garage?'

The clerk shrugged apologetically. 'Best we could do, sir, in the circumstances.'

'Oh, it's unforgivable,' the scholar said. 'He is...'

'Forgiving,' the priest said quickly and smiled at the clerk. 'This garage, my friend. Where is it?'

The garage was in the yard behind the hotel, big enough to house six cars. They hurried towards it and all the arguing about priority was suddenly meaningless. The garage doors were enormous. Wide enough for the three of them to go in together side by side. Wide enough, it seemed, to them, for the whole world to go in.

The little King was cradled in a toolbox lined with a sheepskin car seat cover standing on the fitter's bench. His mother was very young with a strange, unearthly beauty which shone through her tiredness. The man beside her was older. They watched the three visitors warily.

'I am Melchior,' the scholar said courteously and bowed. 'I bring gold to honour the mind of your Son.'

'And I am Balthazar,' the priest said, smiling, 'with incense for his spirit.'

'Caspar,' the red-haired man said gruffly. 'My gift is basil, the sweet-smelling herb with a king's name.'

They placed their gifts on the bench and stood, heads bowed in homage, looking at the King in the toolbox. The King smiled.

'Thank you,' his mother said. 'My little boy is pleased.'

'We are honoured to be here, ma'am.' The voice was a curious amalgam of the priest's and the scholar's but the man who spoke was the red-haired Caspar. But no longer Caspar. Now truly Melthazpar. One man at last, complete and free; mind, body and spirit in harmony, the ancient war within Man finished as the peace of the King entered, healed and made whole.

The young mother picked up the silk sachet of herbs and loosened the gold-tasselled cord. The perfume filled the garage. But it was not the scent of sweet basil. It was the bitter aroma of myrrh.

'You have brought the wrong herb, sir,' she said uncertainly. 'This is no a gift for birth but for burial.' She managed a small, forgiving smile. 'An easy mistake to make, sir. Thank you anyway for the thought behind the gift.'

'I'm sorry,' Melthazpar said, his face suddenly pale, his eyes shadowed. 'I'm very sorry, ma'am. But it is not a mistake.'

She put her hand protectively on her baby, looked up at him, close to tears. 'Not a mistake?'

'No, ma'am,' Melthazpar said gently, sadly. 'It is, I'm afraid, a prophecy.'

And as the dream began to fade I seemed to hear the iron tramp of marching feet and the terrified cries of the mothers of Bethlehem trying to shield their infant sons from Herod's soldiers, and another sound even more threatening, even more ominous. The roar of the mob shouting, 'Crucify'...

By Christmas Day the mantelpiece will be crowded with cards, the one from New Zealand just another pretty piece in the pattern of laughter and love and hope we call Christmas. But when we open our presents on Christmas morning I shall look up at the Magi, the magic men, and remember my dream of that strange, haunted birth touched with splendour, touched with tears.

And I'll be grateful that Christmas leads on to Easter, the promise fulfilled, the fear departed.

Day By Day

DAY BY DAY

The Chairman of our local Hospital Fund-Raising Committee reminds me of a learner bus driver. He only recognizes a stopping place when he has gone past it. We effectively finished the evening's business at 9.45 pm, but at twenty past ten he is still trying to bring the meeting to a close.

'Date of the next meeting, Mr Chairman,' the Secretary says helpfully but with quiet desperation, her habitually pleasant manner beginning to fray round the edges.

"What?' The Chairman blinks. 'Oh yes. Thank you. Please look in your diaries, everyone.'

It seems like a sensible request but it would have puzzled Samuel Pepys who consulted his diary about the past, not about the future.

In his day, of course, a diary was a diary; a large book full of blank pages in which he could scratch away happily for an hour or so every night before closing the entry with that memorable phrase: 'And so to bed.' For him it was a therapeutic exercise conducive to serenity of mind and a calm sleep. But it's not like that for us.

Our diaries are simply pocket-sized calendars packed with so much printed information that our personal contributions are restricted to cryptic notes. *'Dentist at 10 am.'* *'Book Oscar into kennels.'* And, *'Aunt D's birthday'* (heavily underlined because Aunt D is elderly, in uncertain health and wonderfully rich). Not what has been but what is yet to be.

'What about the 6th of next month?' the Chairman says, peering anxiously through the windscreen of his glasses for the welcoming lights of the bus depot, his longed-for journey's end.

Leafing through my diary, I remember an uncle who, had he been born two hundred years earlier, might well have become the Pepys of the Eighteenth Century. He had the same observant eye, the same quirky sense of humour. But his talent withered in the cramped little prison of a seven-days-to-a-page pocket diary (compliments of Smith Bros Furniture Emporium). Day by day, year after year, all he recorded of life's flamboyant parade was the weather. Whenever the conversation flagged he would select an old diary at random from the bookcase beside his chair, open it and announce that eight years ago today the morning was wet and cold but after lunch the sun came out to give a fine evening. To which mind-bending news his wife's invariable response was, 'Food for thought there, dear.'

Remembering his wistful smile as he patted her hand (they were a gentle and devoted couple), I wonder what feasts of wit and erudition he could have conjured up for us had he been given more than a space one inch wide by half an inch deep in which to express himself.

The Secretary says she's sorry she can't manage the 6th but could be free on the 13th. The Chairman stares at her with the eyes of a man betrayed.

I turn the page to find that the 13th is a public holiday in Canada (why is it always Canada in diaries?), a fact I had noted on New Year's Day.

I never feel the year has properly begun until I open my new diary at breakfast on January 1st to check the Canadian holidays, the time of high tide at London Bridge on (say) August 3rd and the telephone number of Aer Lingus. It's just a little ritual I have developed over the years; a sort of crash course in O level General Knowledge and about as useless. I have no intention of flying Aer Lingus to Montreal (or anywhere else) and on the rare occasions I cross London Bridge the tide is always as far out as it can get.

Between mouthfuls of Weetabix I discover when the Hilary law term begins (reassuring in these days of organized crime), summer time ends (depressing) and Oliver Cromwell was born (same date as last year). Over toast and marmalade I move up into the A level bracket. I work out what time it is in Brisbane when it is high noon in Lima, wherever that may be; tell my wife on which day of the week her birthday falls this year and add that Easter will be late again. ('Will Christmas be early, then?' she says sweetly.) I resist the temptation to study the Conversion Tables, the Astronomical Data and hints on First Aid. I like to hold these in reserve to enliven Fund Raising Committee meetings, in the context of which they assume an almost Shakespearian magic.

'Are we all agreed on the 13th, then?' the Chairman says, mentally groping for the handbrake.

But he has reckoned without the Brigadier (rtd) who says that he personally would prefer the 20th, not that it matters, of course. The Treasurer seconds this with almost indecent fervour because it does matter. The Brigadier graciously opens his garden every July for the Grand Summer Fete, our biggest money-raiser. So it matters.

'That's settled then,' the Chairman says with what passes for firmness. 'The 20th of next month it is.'

Everybody nods, missing the Freudian slip, because it isn't the 20th of next month. It's still the 5th of this month (I look at my watch). Just.

The 20th of next month is only a probability, but today is real. Indeed it is the only reality. We can be nostalgic about yesterday, dream about tomorrow, but our ability actually to live is limited to today. This is the secret of successful living; a secret our Chairman (and many like him) fail to understand. He is so busy worrying about tomorrow that he doesn't recognize the enormous opportunities of today until they have slipped through his fingers to become the regrets of yesterday.

But Pepys understood this. He got up every morning, rising from the little death of sleep, not only to a new day but to a whole new lifetime handily gift-wrapped in twenty-four hours. And every night he set it all down in his diary. All the colour, all the pathos, tears to complement the laughter, hope to disarm despair. And so to bed, content in the knowledge that whatever might be waiting for him tomorrow he had lived today to the full.

It's the only way to use a diary. Not to seed the future with anxieties and problems but to reap the harvest each day brings and savour it. 'Take no thought for tomorrow...'

Come to that, it's the only sane way to live.

A Great Past In Front of Me

His name is Henry and he comes from Bradford. A typical Yorkshireman, kind of heart, blunt of speech, loyal to his friends. He brought me a bottle of decent wine on my birthday.

'At your time of life, lad,' he said with his customary directness, 'you want summat as you can enjoy right off. Not summat to keep.'

I grinned. 'Eat, drink and be merry for tomorrow…?'

He shrugged. 'Might as well. You're on the wrong side of sixty now. No future to speak of. Nowt to look forward to, like.'

But there he was mistaken. Not much future, perhaps, but a great past in front of me. For I'm not on the wrong side of sixty, I'm on the heaven-ward side. With the whole of eternity to look forward to.

The years have been good to me. I've climbed up inside the great pyramid of Cheops, sat beside the silent piano in Chopin's house outside Warsaw and been inside Paul Kruger's sitting-room in Pretoria. I've walked a mile or two of Hadrian's Wall and down the Via Dolorosa in Jerusalem, breathed the hot, sulphurous air of the boiling mud pools in Rotorua, New Zealand, and driven the Abraham route from Ur of the Chaldees to Mount Carmel above the Bay of Acre where Elijah had his day of triumph over the prophets of Baal. And I've stood on the crest of Skull Hill outside Jerusalem, picnicked on the shores of Galilee and felt the bite of the winter wind over the brooding grief of Culloden. But always I've had the feeling of being too late—like someone who walks into a theatre to find the play finished and the players long gone. The sets are still there, lovingly preserved but empty and silent. Only the programme notes we call history bear witness to what has been.

What I'm looking forward to now is the timeless, ever-present Now of eternity. Seeing the play as it happens, meeting the players face to face.

Imagine finding Galahad reverently polishing the Grail; the Lady of Shalott restored by grace (to the delight of Tennyson) as Lancelot hoped she might be; and Arthur tweaking Excalibur out of the stone with a quick twist of the wrist while Merlin looks on approvingly. And meeting those Phoenician sea-gypsies who came on a tin-buying cruise to Cornwall with the teenaged Jesus as a cabin boy. Did it really happen, as Blake believed—'And did those feet in ancient time...?'

I want to share a cup of rough Greek wine with those men inside the Trojan Horse, see Midas stuffing himself with saffron cake and watch Icarus learning to pack a parachute designed by Da Vinci. And it will be good to greet Boadicea, liberated after all those years of being stuck in the traffic at the end of Westminster Bridge, her lethal chariot converted to a combine harvester. 'Earth has not anything to show more fair,' Wordsworth said of that view of London. It will be interesting to hear her forthright comments.

Of course, the historians will shrug it all off as being unscholarly nonsense. But I rather think eternity will hold more surprises for historians than for atheists. And, heaven knows, they are in for a rude awakening.

It will be fascinating to eavesdrop on Charles I and Cromwell discussing the divine right of kings tête-à-tête (if you'll forgive the expression) over a glass of nectar bottled in Cana of Galilee; listen to a twentieth-century housewife introducing Alfred the Great to the mysteries of an automatic oven-timer; watch Henry VIII working on the flip side of Greensleeves and hearing Joan of Arc spiritedly putting Bernard Shaw in his place, egged on by Eliza Dolittle.

I'm looking forward to listening to Chaucer telling some of the tales even his publisher refused to print, to discovering what it takes to make John Bunyan laugh and to commiserating with Mark Antony for having to wait so many centuries for Shakespeare to write Caesar's funeral oration for him. And overhearing Adam and Newton discussing original sin with gravity under an apple tree while Eve sits quietly smiling to herself. Not to mention Lazarus comparing notes with Orpheus on the wisdom of taking a return ticket, Vivaldi encouraging J.S. Bach to keep trying, Beethoven listening with pleasure to his own music and Schubert with his symphony finished at last.

Then there's Nebuchadnezzar—the reluctant vegetarian. How much of his foul temper was due to the lack of protein in a diet of grass? And Belshazzar, his profligate son, whose dinner party was ruined by the writing on the wall. If there is graffiti in heaven, will his job be to clean it up?

I once spent a night camping in the ruins of Babylon. Before supper, we walked down the narrow street from the palace, where once a ziggurat planted with flowers and trees, hung like a garden in the sky, to the Water Gate where the royal barge was moored before the river changed its course in the Great Flood which gave us the story of Noah and his floating zoo. Now there's a man I want to talk to, preferably in the company of Charles Darwin, and ask him whatever happened to unicorns.

But Babylon was magic. I felt the centuries telescope when the stars came out over the desert and the shadows between the decorated walls became Nebuchadnezzar's people, lively ghosts crowding that ancient, empty stage. We lit a small fire to cook our supper and remembered Shadrach and his two fireproof friends. They are high on my list of men I want to meet. I shall ask them about that fourth man who was with them in the heart of that burning, fiery furnace to keep them unharmed and put fear into the heart of the king.

Not that I'll need to ask, of course. He will be there in person, welcoming, forgiving, understanding. Legend and fact will be swallowed up in truth, all the questions answered, all the riddles solved. And seeing him moving freely, easily among us, as once he did in Nazareth and Jerusalem (and perhaps Glastonbury), I'll know I have found my way back home at last...

As though reading my thoughts, Henry raised his glass. 'Many happy returns, lad,' he said, his eyes gently sardonic.

'Thank you, Henry,' I said. 'I'll drink to that.'

A FRIEND INDEED

Alarm clocks (unlike children) should be seen and heard. Ours scores A for Achievement on both counts. Built like a clockwork bomb, he has a black face, luminous hands, a tick like a trip-hammer and a bell to split the sky. I say He because he is far too strong a personality to be a mere It. We call him Hans—as in the song: *You Need Han(d)s*. We certainly do.

Over the years Hans and I have evolved an integrated relationship in which I am an equal (though sleeping) partner. I need him to waken me on time, he needs me to wind up and activate his sturdy mechanism. Such mutual dependence is the surest foundation of friendship.

And that is what he is, an old-fashioned, reliable, family friend.

Opening a sleepy eye in the small hours, it is infinitely reassuring to hear that iron heartbeat, see that round, honest face peering benignly at me from the bedside table. I give him a grateful smile and drift contentedly back to sleep again until the bell goes off like a fire engine arriving through the bedroom wall. Not that it often comes to that. In common with most alarm clock owners, I have developed a sixth sense which wakens me precisely three seconds before the bell; just sufficient time to pat Hans gently on the head and cancel his call. If he finds this frustrating he is careful not to show it, tactfully disclaiming all credit for getting me up on time.

They say that familiarity breeds contempt. My partnership with Hans mocks such cynicism. Like all true friendships, ours has matured with age. And that's the trouble. The gradual ageing process which has dimmed my eye has also faded his luminous paint. I was beginning to find it difficult to distinguish between his hour hand and his minute hand and would wake with a start at a quarter to three, under the impression that it was a quarter past nine. An unnerving experience with which to start the day. 'What we need,' Sheena said, 'is a new clock.'

I looked at her with dismay. She was right, of course. My wife usually is. But—get rid of Hans? It was unthinkable. An act of betrayal neither of us could perpetrate.

And then, out of the blue, our hands were forced. Sally Fletcher rang.

Acquaintances rather than friends, the Fletchers are well-to-do (two bathrooms, two cars, two acres), able to afford a winter holiday abroad in addition to a summer one. But pleasant with it.

'We're flying from Luton this time, you see,' Sally said over the phone. 'And the thing is, we have to be at the airport at seven in the morning. Which would mean leaving home at two. Such a bore.'

I agreed, visualizing a fogbound M1 at two o'clock on a November morning.

'It's an awful cheek,' she said, 'and please do say if it's not convenient. But we were wondering—could you possibly put us up overnight?'

It made sense. At that time we were living only thirty minutes drive from Luton. 'Of course you must come,' I said. 'Our pleasure.'

They insisted on dining en route and arrived just before ten that evening. We spent a pleasant hour chatting over bedtime drinks.

'No need for you to get up in the morning,' Peter Fletcher said. 'We'll get breakfast at the airport.' He brushed our protests aside, a polite man but big. Not to be trifled with. 'If we could just borrow an alarm? Sorry to be a nuisance but we're both heavy sleepers and...'

So I gave them Hans, all wound up and set for five-thirty a.m.

'Oh, quaint,' Sally said. 'I haven't seen one of those for absolutely ages.'

Her husband explained suavely that they had a digital clock radio. 'Figures instead of hands, y'know.'

'Yes,' I said (I did actually know that). 'Well, you'll find that old gentleman very reliable.'

'I'm sure,' he said doubtfully, his hands quivering slightly under the power of that massive heartbeat. 'Only... well, you'll think us terribly fussy, but we're not used to a clock ticking in the bedroom.'

'You won't be able to sleep?' Sheena said.

'Not a wink, I'm afraid,' Sally said.

'Sorry,' Peter said.

Which is why Hans got me up at five-thirty the next morning to take them in a cup of tea. And why, later that day, we went out and bought a digital clock radio.

There followed three miserable months of restless nights and guilt-ridden days with Hans silent and abandoned in a cupboard.

Oh, the new gadget was easy to see; a brilliant digital display glowing with radioactive rays, almost bright enough to read by. And waking up to music is less traumatic than old Hans's manic fire bell. But I missed that driving, remorseless tick and the changing (but always friendly) expression on that familiar black face as the hands slowly revolved from supper to breakfast.

And the new clock had a mind of its own. One night the radio switched itself on at three a.m. and played heavy rock at us for twenty horrendous minutes while I frantically pushed buttons and twiddled knobs before finally managing to silence it by pulling the plug out of the wall socket (and oversleeping until nine). I don't know why it did that. I read the instruction book (in four languages, one of which bore a faint resemblance to English) again the next morning and I still don't know why.

Nor was it always music which infiltrated our dreams. I can think of no more discouraging way to greet the morning than to hear a disembodied voice saying, '... early sunshine will soon give way to heavy showers, prolonged at times, with a chance of snow on high ground.' Especially in May.

But it was the hands I really missed; those faintly glowing, friendly little pointers creating patterns I have known and understood since childhood. If I waken around ten to seven they tell me instantly that I have time in hand. Time to sleep a little longer or yawn and stretch and come fully awake. Civilized. But the digital display, flashing its curt 06.48, reduces me to a clumsy computer being activated by a code. Demeaning.

'We'll soon get used to it, I suppose,' Sheena said doubtfully after the first week without Hans.

'Of course we will,' I said, horribly afraid that we would.

Praise God, we haven't, nor now ever shall. Because the DCR has been banished to the guest room (in case the Fletchers should come again) and Hans is back in his rightful place beside the bed, his brave old heart pounding away, his black face forgiving.

A retrograde step? I wonder. They say horses are coming back. And open fires. So why not proper alarm clocks?

Every night I wind up Hans and dare to believe he is a symbol of hope. A reassurance that the old virtues still have a place in our gimmick-ridden society. An affirmation that when our children have grown weary of cheap plastic values (as they surely will, being hungry for truth and stability) there will be honour still, and loyalty and love for them to rediscover with delight.

ROMANCE HAS MANY FACES

R omance has many faces but my father's was not noticeably one of them. My mother's was. She was a Scot, dark-eyed, softly-spoken, with all the piquant charm of her race. Her given name was Mary but my father called her Polly. He was not a demonstrative man and avoided words of endearment. Perhaps Polly was his synonym for Darling. I like to think so.

He was a building contractor in Manchester. Blunt-featured and dogmatic, with bright red hair and a temper to match, he was as hard-headed as the bowler hat he habitually wore to the office. Scrupulously honest, opinionated, proud—yes, all of these. But romantic? My father? As well call Frank Muir dull, Madonna modest. And yet...

Sixty years ago, when I had just started at the Grammar School and there really was nothing over sixpence in Woolworth's, he invited my mother and me to accompany him on a walk after lunch on Easter Saturday. A fine April day it was and he raffish in holiday attire—navy-blue suit, white shirt, no waistcoat. Shedding his waistcoat was the nearest he ever got to casual dress, even on the beach.

'A walk?' My mother marked her surprise. My father was not one to go walking just for something to do. 'Where to?'

'Up the hill,' he said briskly. 'Down through the village. Back along the towpath.' He took out his gold pocket watch (he considered wrist watches to be effeminate and unreliable). 'Ready in ten minutes, please.'

All my father's invitations were like that. Formal, peremptory, detailed. People who didn't know him well frequently mistook them for commands.

My mother went upstairs to get ready. He looked meaningfully at my shoes. 'You know where we keep the shoe polish, my son,' he said.

I cleaned my shoes, washed my hands, reported for inspection and was sent back to brush my hair properly. My mother came down, delicious in a small round hat, jacket and skirt, pearl-buttoned blouse, soft leather gloves. My father smiled proudly and said to me, 'When gentlemen are privileged to escort a lady, they honour her by looking their best.'

'Yes, Dad.' It seemed to me entirely reasonable then. And still does.

We lived on a small estate of semis which backed on to a wood beside the golf course. I collected lost golf balls the way other boys collected conkers. But more profitably. Our house was called Linkside. My father was not an imaginative man.

Driving back there recently, I was appalled by its shabby monotony; the broken fences, the littered gardens, the vandalized road signs. But in the Thirties it was all fresh and green, an escape from the soot-stained terraces of the inner suburbs.

There was a pathway through the wood and we walked up past the old Bishop's Palace, now a private nursing home, into another world. Fine, solid houses stood in their own grounds behind hedges of ornamental privet. The gravel drives were raked clean. The sun shone through the new-leafed trees. Birds sang. There were daffodils, not spaced out in meagre rows as in our own tiny flower beds, but scattered in great golden drifts across lawns as vast as an East Anglian field. It was very quiet; a warm, expensive stillness.

Walking beneath a flowering cherry, my mother took a deep breath. 'Will you smell that perfume.'

My father smiled his hard, bricks-and-mortar smile. 'That's money, Polly. No smell like it this side of heaven.'

'Och, you.' My mother shook her head, smiling. 'You're aboot as romantic as a bank statement, so you are.'

At the top of the hill where the road forked we turned right towards the village.

'It's along here somewhere,' my father said, carefully casual.

She looked at him quickly. 'What is?'

'The house.'

'What house is that?'

'The Larches,' my father said, the patience in his voice beginning to stretch a little. 'The house my client wants me to look at for him. He bought it last week. Got it for a song.'

'What's the matter with it?'

'Nothing much. Just wants doing up a bit. I'm to give him an estimate.'

My mother sighed. 'Aye,' she said resignedly. 'I might ha'e guessed it was business we're on.'

My father raised an eyebrow. 'You didn't think we'd trail all the way up here just for the exercise, did you?'

'No' for one moment,' my mother said.

'Well then,' my father said.

The road was a tunnel of trees; big, mature trees. Oaks and elms and the occasional horse chestnut. Not a larch in sight. I looked at the names carved on the stone gate posts. The Limes. Birch Villa. Pine Woods. I began to laugh.

'What's so funny?' my father said suspiciously. He considered laughter to be an extravagance, except in the music hall.

'The house names,' I said. 'They're all wrong.'

'How?' my mother said.

I explained.

'Is that what they teach you at school?' my father said incredulously. 'The names of trees?'

'Yes, Dad.'

He sniffed. 'Flowers too, I suppose?'

'And birds.'

'Hmm.' He compressed his lips. 'I suppose it's relevant. To ploughmen and gardeners. Is that what you want to be?'

'I don't think so.'

'There's more to education than the three R's,' my mother said.

'So they tell me.' My father's voice was heavy with disbelief. 'But you don't need to be a botanist to build houses. What goes under a concrete path?'

But I was expecting that and ready for it. 'Hard core. Broken bricks, rubble, stones.'

'I know what hard core is, my son. What's five per cent?'

I was expecting that too. 'A shilling in the pound.'

My mother laughed. 'You see?'

'Hmm,' my father said. And, perhaps because it was Easter, left it there.

About a hundred yards further on we came to The Larches; an old Victorian villa standing forlorn in an unkempt garden. Its wooden gate, bearing the irrelevant name, sagged on a broken hinge beside an overgrown holly bush. My father half-pushed, half-lifted it open and stood aside for my mother.

'It's no' this one, surely?' she said.

I looked at the mottled bricks, the broken slates on the roof, the old-fashioned sash windows streaked with dirt and bird droppings, the peeling paint, the tangled weeds. I knew what she was feeling. After our bright little semi this was something out of Dickens.

'I told you it needed doing up,' my father said huffily.

My mother made a face. 'Or pulling down.'

He unlocked the front door with a massive key and pushed it open. We peered into the dark hall. There was a musty, sickly smell. 'Watch your step, now,' my father said. 'There's a touch of dry rot here.'

Which was something of an understatement. There was a hole in the hall floor you could have dropped a sideboard through. My mother said faintly, 'What's doon there?'

'Cellars,' my father said succinctly.

'I didna suppose it was the bathroom,' she said, bridling at his tone.

'Good,' he said. 'Because there isn't one. Yet.' He opened an inner door. 'This is the drawing room.'

It was tall and square, ugly as a lift shaft. Dirt-encrusted paper hung in tatters from the walls and ceiling. The fireplace gaped at us, a huge, black mouth toothless in a face of diseased marble. My father stamped heavily across the floor, raising a cloud of dust. 'This is sound enough.'

'I'm awfu' glad o' that,' my mother said flatly.

The dining-room was no better. Its tatty fireplace was, if anything, even worse. I looked out of the warped window at the back garden; a jungle of rank grass, nettles and raspberry canes run wild. My father stamped about happily, his shoes speckled with flakes of fallen plaster. He was in his element, undismayed by the blotchy wallpaper, the broken picture rails, the scabrous paint. Seeing only the firm, strong bones beneath the withered skin, the true nature of the house as it had once been, as it could become again.

'Look at these proportions,' he said admiringly. 'They don't build houses like this any more.'

'I'm relieved tae hear it,' my mother said tartly.

We went down the gloomy hall into a third room. Part of the ceiling had collapsed. My mother stared at the pile of plaster and torn paper on the floor. 'What's this, then?' she said. 'A midden?'

'This is the morning room,' my father said a shade pompously.

She shivered. 'That'll be mourning wi' a U, forbye,' she said.

My father's mouth tightened. 'It's not that bad.'

'Och, it's dreadful,' my mother said. 'Ye ken fine it is.'

He shrugged and led the way into the kitchen.

The kitchen was a nightmare. Compared with it, the other rooms were straight out of the Ideal Homes Exhibition. It had a stone floor, very uneven, a cracked stone sink full of dead spiders and an enormous rusted iron range. My mother stared at it in horror. Even my father blinked a little. There was something sinister about that range. It was like an altar to some latter-day Lancastrian Moloch, built for human sacrifices.

'Bit of work needed in here,' my father said bravely. The range grinned at him evilly with rusty iron teeth.

Upstairs, the bedrooms had clearly been designed to die in. Long, lingering, Victorian-style deaths, the sufferer in a huge, mahogany bed surrounded by weeping children and grandchildren. My father pointed out that three of the four bedrooms would get the morning sun. My mother was not impressed by this information. Nor was I. It seemed to me unlikely that anyone rash enough to sleep in them would survive to see the morning. I understood now the significance of the wide staircase. It had been designed to take a brass-handled coffin comfortably.

There were two attics on the second floor, with sloping ceilings and dormer windows. They smelt strongly of mice.

As we trooped thankfully downstairs again, my father stroked the banister rail with a hand as sensitive as a sculptor's. 'Beautiful,' he said quietly, almost reverently.

We stood by the raspberry canes in the back garden while he explored the outbuildings, one of which contained the only lavatory. My mother held my hand, as much to comfort herself as to reassure me.

Walking home (every step an escape from horror into familiar comfort) my mother said, 'Is your client married at a'?'

'Yes. Why?'

'Och, the puir woman,' my mother said. 'I dinna envy her. A house like yon…'

'You don't like it?' There was something in my father's voice, like a snagged thread. Impatience, perhaps? Anxiety? I wondered if, having advised his client to buy the house, he was now regretting it.

'Like it?' my mother said. 'It's terrible. It hasna' got a thing gaeing for it.'

My father looked grim, saying nothing. I watched him covertly. Was it possible that this omniscient man could make a mistake? I found the idea at once disquieting and, in a curious way, heart-warming. I felt suddenly very close to him, the discovery of his feet of clay transforming my respectful hero-worship into love. 'My father will fix it, you'll see,' I said, more loyal than believing.

'Aye,' my mother said sadly. 'Mebbe. That's what the clansmen said aboot Bonnie Charlie, ye ken. And look what happened tae him, puir laddie.'

My father smiled and winked at me.

A couple of weeks later he brought home a pile of catalogues. Fireplaces, tiled kitchen ranges with back boilers, electric cookers, sink units, bathroom suites.

'What's all this, then?' my mother said. 'No' for here, surely?'

'No. For The Larches. My client's given us the work. It's to be a surprise for his wife.'

'Och, she'll be surprised wi' yon ruin. Shocked, mair like.'

My father shrugged. 'Anyway, he's anxious to get a woman's opinion about the fittings. He can't very well ask his wife, so he's asked me to get your advice.'

My mother looked doubtful and a little pleased. 'I canna dae that. Everyone's taste is no' the same.'

'Yours is excellent. Just a few pointers, Polly. Please.'

'Well...' She opened a catalogue and was hooked.

'Take your time now,' he said. 'And don't worry about the prices. He got the house so cheaply he can afford to splash out a bit.'

'It's a'richt for some,' my mother said.

The next week it was wallpaper samples. The week after, carpets and curtains. And a pound box of chocolates.

'From my client,' my father said. 'A little token of appreciation. He's very taken with your choice so far.'

Whit Monday was sunny that year. In the morning my father cut the lawn and we had our lunch out in the garden. Afterwards he said casually, 'Fancy a walk? Only The Larches is all finished. The new owner and his wife'll be moving in sometime next week. I thought you might like to see what we've made of it.'

'You're sure he won't mind?' my mother said.

My father sighed. 'Do you want to see it or don't you?'

'Yes.'

'Well, then.'

The first thing we noticed was the new gate. It was painted white with the name of the house picked out in black letters. The name was new, too. Now it was called Holly House.

My father pointed to the holly bush beside it, trim and neat now. 'Right?'

I nodded. 'Yes, Dad.'

The garden had been transformed, the lawn cut and shaped, the drive widened, the hedge trimmed. The front door had been stripped and oiled to bring up the natural grain of the wood. There was a large new casement window in the drawing-room. The brickwork was freshly pointed, the roof tiled, the gutters and down-spouts renewed.

'Handsome, eh?' my father said.

'Aye,' my mother said.

Inside, it was a different house. The redecorated rooms were light and airy, gracefully spacious and welcoming. My mother had chosen well. Colours toned and matched, fireplaces complementing curtains, carpets contrasting pleasantly with the wallpapers. One of the first floor bedrooms had become a bathroom, tiled and mirrored. Above, under the roof, the attics were now a study and bedroom suite complete with built-in bookshelves and a splendid writing-table.

But it was the kitchen which was really unrecognizable. Gone were the old stone sink, the dreadful iron-toothed range. The flagged floor was now rubber tiled and warm. The new sink was a poem in white and chromium, the new range, tiled and neat, invited the cooking of magnificent meals. Everything smelled fresh and clean.

'It's like a miracle, so it is,' my mother said, standing in the hall which was filled with light now thanks to a new window in the end wall. The door into the dining-room was open. Through the window, the back garden was as neat as the front. Above us, the staircase rose grandly, its width now conjuring visions, not of coffins being carried out, but of smiling guests coming down to breakfast from those sun-in-the-morning bedrooms.

'Well, Polly,' my father said. 'What d'you think?'

My mother shook her head in wonder. 'Och, it's marvellous, so it is. A bonnie, bonnie house.'

'You really like it?' he said with a hint of anxiety.

'Like it? I can hardly believe it's real.'

My father put his hands in his trouser pockets and leaned comfortably against the carved newel post at the foot of the stairs. 'That's good,' he said quietly, 'because it's yours, my dear.'

'Mine?' My mother's eyes opened wide. 'But how? I mean, your client...'

'To my knowledge,' my father said, 'there's nothing to prevent a man taking instructions from himself.'

She swallowed. 'You mean you...?'

'I bought it and did it up for you, Polly. It's in your name.'

'You darlin' man.' My mother put her arms round his neck and kissed him. 'And all these weeks, here I've been thinking it was a' for someone else.'

My father smiled. 'A present's not a present unless it's a surprise.'

Looking back over the years between, I can still see them standing there in each other's arms, caught in a timeless moment of pleasure, my father's hair like a flame in the sunlight, tears of happiness in my mother's eyes. And on their faces, the open secret of love demonstrated and requited.

Romantic? My father?

My mother thought so.

TUPPENCE COLOURED

The old rhyme about roses and violets is wrong. Roses are not red but a gorgeous velvety black. White too, of course, and occasionally blue but never red. Not for me. I'm colour blind.

This means I belong to a privileged minority (almost exclusively male) for whom winter skies are a cheerful pink and summer skies royal purple. Not surprisingly, we tend to be optimists.

My friends, who have to make do with what is arrogantly called normal colour vision, tend to be amused that I see pink horses (the old grey mare she ain't what they think she is). Pink elephants too, without the misery of a hangover. Not to mention green cocker spaniels (Golden? A *gold* dog? You can't be serious), green pillar boxes and green fire-engines. But not green traffic lights. The Go light is white, the Stop light brown. Red? That's the one in the middle.

Amusement turns to sympathy when people discover I have difficulty in seeing holly berries because they are the same colour as the leaves. And to envy because my bank account may be overdrawn on occasions but is never in the red. And sometimes to indignation, as when I rashly told a girl how much I admired her green hair. She was a redhead with a temper to match. I have not made that mistake again.

There are times when the amusement is mine. In my world a change of shade, too subtle for those with standard colour vision, often means a change of colour. It can be a very useful weapon.

Invited to speak at a ladies' luncheon club, I was warned by my agent to beware of the secretary, whom he described as being a high-born lady with a poor opinion of men in general and male speakers in particular. He was right. She met me in the vestibule, tall, cool of voice, impeccably groomed. She was wearing an expensively tailored skirt and jacket over a finely-knitted wool jumper, with the inevitable rope of (real) pearls. Daddy was obviously a brigadier (rtd), her husband a half-colonel and still rising.

'Mr Jackson?' She raised one arched eyebrow.

'Jackman,' I said.

'What?'

'My name is Jackman, not Jackson.' It is something I have spent half a life-time explaining.

'So sorry.' She turned to the President and introduced me as, 'Mr Chapman.' It wasn't that she was deaf, just supremely uninterested.

The President gave me her hand. She was small and fluttery, with a nice smile. I liked her. 'So glad you could come, Mr Jackman.'

The secretary shrugged impatiently and led the way into the luncheon room through a throng of women, pausing here and there to spread a little sunshine with remarks like,

'You don't look terribly well to me, Dorothy,' and, 'Mavis, how nice to see you again. You must let me give you the name of my hairdresser sometime.'

Charming, I thought. If this is how she treats her friends, what hope have I got?

But when we reached the top table everything changed.

'It's impossibly stuffy in here,' the secretary said and unbuttoned her jacket. I looked with astonished delight at her jumper.

'I love that jumper, dear,' the President said. 'Did you knit it yourself?'

'Oh yes. I never buy machine-knitted woollens.'

'It's beautifully done,' the President said. 'Such a pretty shade of green.'

I had suspected that since it looked red to me. But not all of it. Two thirds of the way down, she had run out of wool and bought some more. But she had not quite managed a perfect match, because the lower part of the jumper was not red but brown. Even more fascinatingly, the colour changed in the middle of a row. She didn't know this, nor did the President. Nor anyone else in the room, for that matter. Except me.

'Don't you agree?' the President said to me.

'Very striking,' I said with a smile. The wonder was that I didn't laugh out loud. 'Most unusual.'

The secretary heard the new note of confidence in my voice and looked at me sharply. I met her gaze with calm superiority. She was no longer awe-inspiring, merely ridiculous. She frowned, uneasily aware that our roles had been suddenly reversed to give me the upper hand; at a loss to understand how this had come about.

I didn't enlighten her.

Only the colour blind realize how often colours are used in casual conversation and what problems they can cause.

'I'm looking for a bookshop,' I say to a passer-by in an unfamiliar town.

'Quince Lane, off New Street,' he says. 'Down on the left. Second turning. Or is it the third? Anyway, there's a house on the corner with a yellow door. You can't miss it.'

Not true.

At the wedding reception, the man standing beside me said, 'Who's that gorgeous woman in the blue hat?'

'No idea,' I said automatically.

But when my wife in her new hat came over to me a little later, slipped her arm comfortably through mine and said, 'Enjoying yourself, darling?' he gave me a very old-fashioned look.

Broadcasting the Radio 4 morning service some years ago, I set the scene for the listeners with a brief description of the church, mentioning the red roses on the communion table and the white Peace roses round the fountain outside. I had prudently checked on the red ones beforehand but not the white ones. I have no trouble with white.

Afterwards, a member of my congregation said, 'Well done, Stuart. Great service.' He lowered his voice. 'The only thing is, Peace roses are pink.'

Then there is this wretched modern habit of colour coding. I hate to think how much time I have wasted in hotel bathrooms over the years, waiting for the cold tap (marked with a coloured disc instead of a sensible C) to run hot. And how often, visiting members of my congregation in hospital, I have arrived at the wrong ward after following the green stripe on the floors of endless corridors under the impression that it was a brown one. And waited impatiently for my wife to come home from the shops and solve for me the problem of which wire goes where in a standard three-pin plug.

The choice of a wife is important to a colour blind man who has had to rely, all his unmarried years, upon his mother to guide him in his purchase of ties, socks and suits. Fortunately, very few women are colour blind. I don't suppose (unless you are one of us) you have ever put on a red tie with a green pullover, brown trousers and taupe socks, believing them to be a perfect match. I have. And was sent back upstairs by my incredulous wife to change.

But these are minor irritations; a small price to pay for living in a world of bold, flamboyant colours—discounting all those pallid pastels beloved of interior decorators, which I see only as off-white. A world of brilliant green fire, pink-slated roofs and golden lawns, where the bright yellow leaves of April mellow to a gentle green in the autumn and the winter snow reflects the soft pink of a January sky. Plus the fact that colour blind eyes can see like a cat's in the dark; a compensatory factor which does wonders for our electricity bills.

I am also grateful that God spares a thought for the colour blind among his children. His rainbow sign of forgiveness is as vivid (though different) to me as to you. And he sent the resurrection angels to the empty tomb dressed in brilliant white—the one colour (besides black) which we all see the same. I find this one more proof of his care, who is Father to us all and discriminates against none.

They say the superb artist, Turner, was painting outdoors late one afternoon when a lady peered over his shoulder at the canvas and said patronizingly, 'And what is that supposed to be?'

'The sunset, madam,' Turner said with remarkable self-control.

'Oh, really? Well, I've never seen a sunset like that.'

'No, madam,' Turner said. 'But don't you wish you had?'

I know exactly what he meant.

BEWARE OF EXPERTS

I am considering founding a Society for the Abolition of
Experts (SAE).

The initials also stand for Stamped Addressed
Envelope. This is a happy coincidence because the stamped
addressed envelope is a typical expert's ploy. It immediately
emphasizes that you are consulting a person of superior
intelligence who cannot be expected to fuss with stamps
and addresses. His mind is on higher things. Like money.

Some people work for a wage, others (more grandly) for
a salary. Experts charge a fee (plus expenses). The only
thing they have to sell is their time. But, as you and your
bank manager will quickly discover, they have no sense of
time and cannot be hurried; a characteristic they share with
British Rail, local council employees and people in public
telephone boxes. This is because they habitually reject the

obvious and search with agonizing slowness for the obscure. Consulting an expert is simply an expensive way of shelving a problem. By the time he comes up with an answer (not necessarily the right one), the problem will have solved itself, one way or another.

So experts don't come cheaply. They don't, actually, come at all if they can avoid it, for it is easier to pretend to wisdom in a letter (and finally a report) than face to face. Hence the classic definition of an expert as being an ordinary person a long way from home. The nearer you get to him (or her) the more unimpressive he becomes. Prophets are said to have the same problem.

A glance at your television screen (it is seldom worth more these days) will confirm that experts adopt a variety of disguises. They can be suave in Saville Row suits and gold-rimmed spectacles, tweedily intellectual with leather patches on the elbows of their jackets, or freakish with extraordinary hair and odd socks. However, they are not difficult to identify. All you have to do is get them to talk. This is all too easy. All experts are compulsive talkers, fascinated by the sound of their own voices. They give themselves away not, as you might imagine, by what they say (the content of their speeches is ferociously dull) but by the way they say it.

Where you or I would say, 'Yes', experts invariably say, 'Definitely', or (oddly) 'Perhaps'. 'In fact' is always, 'In actual fact', 'Now' expanded to, 'At this moment in time'. After five minutes of their conversation you realize why they are so expensive.

When they want to put you in your place (below them) they say, 'With respect', or more insidiously, 'With the greatest possible respect'. They do not, of course, apologize. Sentences which begin, 'I'm sorry, but...' are their way of telling you how wrong you are. They themselves are never wrong. Misunderstood, perhaps. But never wrong.

It is important to distinguish between an expert and a professional. Professionals—doctors, teachers, accountants and (some) economists—are well-qualified, highly-trained and reassuringly competent. They have expertise but they are not experts in the accepted meaning of the word. When confronted with a particularly silly idea, they smile and shrug and say, 'We'll leave that to the experts, shall we?'

Experts, like Members of Parliament (which they so often become) have no specific training for anything. They are broadly-based and open-ended, reminiscent of those old, hand-cranked mincing machines our grandmothers used. You feed them problems instead of the remains of the Sunday joint, but the general principle is the same. What goes in as a simply stated question emerges greatly increased in volume, a convoluted mass of jargon compressed into a twenty-four page report, each page of which has taken a month to produce. If you have the stamina to plough through it, you will discover that experts, like fortune-tellers, can only tell you what you have already told them, but more expensively. They do not create; they recycle. It is their mission in life to make a bad job worse. And at this they excel.

Every woman knows that her favourite recipe for lemon meringue pie, which has established her among her circle of friends as being a magnificent cook, will cruelly betray her without warning an hour before a dinner-party designed to ensure her husband's promotion to a seat on the board of his firm. She prepares the ingredients with meticulous care, checks that the oven is at exactly the right temperature and pops the pie in, serenely confident that it will be a masterpiece. But this time—this one, hyper-important time—it comes out a gooey, unappetizing ruin even the cat rejects.

Nobody knows why this should be. It's just something we have to live with, like wet Bank Holidays, Michael Jackson and people selling double-glazing on the doorstep.

It is also the kind of traumatic disaster on which experts thrive. But if our unfortunate hostess, tearfully opening a tin of pears, is ill-advised enough to consult an expert, his long-delayed answer (suitably translated) will be: 'You should have made the pie the week before and put it in the freezer.'

It's answers like this which cry out for my Society.

If an individual expert can seriously damage your peace of mind, a group of them can utterly destroy it.

A modern version of the parable of the Good Samaritan might well begin: 'A certain motorist went down from London to Brighton and fell among experts...' It's happened to all of us; the unexpected breakdown on a busy main road which delivers us into the hands of the experts.

There is always a middle-aged man, trying to recapture his youth in a vintage sports car, who talks authoritative rubbish about big ends. A nineteen-year-old enthusiast with a bewildering assortment of tools in the boot of his self-assembled old banger who is all for dismantling the gearbox to free the drive shaft. A passing farmer in a mud-spattered Land Rover who has to be forcibly discouraged from hammering a nail through the fuel pipe to clear an (imaginary) air lock. And the inevitable humorist (of all experts the most unnerving) who asks you if you have thought of putting petrol in the tank? They appear at the drop of a spanner, like vultures round a dying animal, and I have long suspected that they are hired jointly by the AA and the RAC to boost membership.

But they are angels of mercy compared with a group of religious experts; Gentlemen and (increasingly) Ladies of the Cloth who sit on ecclesiastical committees and issue portentous pronouncements of alarming naivety on matters of the Faith. Mild of manner, well-meaning and verbose, their only qualifications appear to be a vocabulary so specialized that it is incomprehensible to the public at large, a disquieting compulsion to heresy and a total ignorance of the hopes and fears of ordinary folk. If you think that the average parliamentary debate (as seen on TV) is notable only for its overweening complacency you should eavesdrop on a religious debate at any level— parish, diocese or national Synod. But only if you are sure of what you believe. And are forgiving towards bishops.

To boost the membership of my SAE I shall offer a year's free subscription to whomever comes up with the best collective noun for experts. A number of possibilities spring immediately to mind. An Encumbrance, perhaps, or an Exclusion (they all live in ivory towers, remote from reality). An Infestation would be apt, for they are all parasites living comfortably on our worries and fears.

Of course, there's always the word 'Panel'. Did you know that in Scottish law a panel means an accused person or persons?

It will surely take an expert to better that.

BROWNIE POINTS

They come in the halcyon hour between school and tea, flitting up the path like owlets in their Brownie uniforms, clutching small folders each containing a letter, a poem and a story carefully set out in their best handwriting.

Perching solemnly on the big settee, they watch me begin to read, their eyes round with apprehension.

Jane's granny has sent her an anorak for her birthday and she has replied with a note of thanks, with a snippet of news (Alice is going to have a family). It ends simply and splendidly with one word: Love.

I smile at her. 'Who's Alice?'

'Our spaniel.'

'And how is she?'

'Fat.'

They all giggle delightedly, the ice broken.

'It's a good letter, Jane,' I say, meaning it. After all, if they had had anoraks in Shakespeare's day the chances are he would have spelled it 'annorrack' too.

Emily (1)'s poem scans but doesn't rhyme. They seem not to teach rhyming verse now, apparently believing ideas should not be corseted in the discipline of a rhyme scheme. Which is rather like eating with your fingers because knives and forks demand skills that have to be learned. A pity. Emily's ideas are worth shaping.

> *'I sometimes think*
> *the world's a cube*
> *of sugar in God's*
> *cup of tea...'*

An astonishing opening and if she lacks the experience to develop it, that will come in time. I look at her with respect. 'You've got an extremely good imagination, Emily.'

'I know,' she says politely. 'Mummy says it's because I'm a Libra.'

'Really?' I say, wishing Mummy had more sense.

Emily (2) (what is the fascination of Victorian housemaids' names for today's sophisticated parents?) has written a story which is almost a film script; strong on action, weak on description. The writing is economical, almost curt, the events derivative. It starts in a Devon farmhouse (Enid Blyton) and finishes with high drama in the middle of a river in the Scottish Highlands (R.L.Stevenson). In between, we visit a corner shop (Coronation Street), find a lost dog (Juliet Bravo), take a helicopter ride (Anneka Rice) and cook a meal (Clement Freud). And all this in three pages from a school exercise book.

There are the inevitable technical faults. 'It's' and 'Its' tend to be interchangeable and people lay down as often as they lie down. But the thrust of the story is compelling. It has a beginning, a middle (well, a large variety of middles, actually) and an end. Which is refreshingly old-fashioned.

'How long have you been writing stories, Emily?'

'Oh, ages,' she says, reminding me that when you are eight a month is a long, long time.

'Do you like doing it?'

'No,' she says firmly. A remark of such devastating honesty that I can find no answer to it. Except to award her her Writer's badge along with Jane and Emily (l).

They breathe a concerted sigh of relief and ease themselves back a little on the settee, exchanging triumphant smiles.

Going for the double (Writer's and Reader's) they have brought lists of books they have read. Gratifyingly long lists even when dubious entries like *June Annual* and *Choosing and Caring for Your Rabbit* are disregarded.

Jane's list features *Black Beauty*, set in a world I can only just remember and she has never seen. But there is a mysterious rapport between little girls and horses and she talks with breathless pleasure about that moralistic sentimental story of heroism and loyalty and kindness in unexpected places—qualities which are as immortal as they are dated. 'I like the part where the doctor's called out at night in a storm,' I say, just to check she has read the book.

'Oh, yes.' Her eyes shine. 'In the gig.'

'Our doctor plays the guitar,' Emily (2) announces brightly.

Emily (1) promptly dissolves in helpless laughter.

'Not that kind of gig, stupid,' Jane says scathingly.

Emily (1) is heavily into Beatrix Potter. I pick a title at random and ask her what it's about. She licks her lips and launches into a labyrinth of she-said-and-then-they-said narrative, further confused by phrases like: 'Oh, before that there was this man who...' and: 'Only that bit comes later after...'

I don't attempt to follow it (I've been here before many times). I just sit and enjoy her enthusiasm.

'You like rabbits, do you?' I say when she finally runs out of words.

She nods eagerly, pony-tail jiggling, face pink with pleasure.

'My Mum makes them into pies,' Jane says tactlessly.

I break the shocked silence by asking Emily (2) for her list. It reads like a publisher's catalogue for Enid Blyton and A.A. Milne into which have strayed two outsiders: *A Christmas Carol* and the Bible (or, as Emily meticulously calls it, The Holy Bible). I mentally toss a coin between Tiny Tim and Pooh. It comes down for Tim. So off we go with Scrooge and Marley's ghost in a condensed version which would be the envy of the Reader's Digest and the despair of Dickens, who never used one word when six would do.

'Well done, Emily,' I say when she eventually arrives at 'God bless us, every one.' 'And do you really read your Bible?'—suspecting an ambitious mother in the background playing her trump card for the impressionable parson.

Emily (2) looks at me, her eyes considering. She has grey eyes and dark, curly hair and will probably give her parents sleepless nights before she is very much older. She smiles apologetically. 'Only the good bits,' she says demurely.

I sign their badge warrants, making a production of it as befits the occasion, open the door and watch them go skipping away down the path to the waiting cars. There will be celebrations tonight, crisps and coke for tea and perhaps a ceremonial sewing-on of their badges. And when they meet on Friday evening, Brown Owl will be suitably impressed.

One of my scholarly friends says the whole exercise is a misuse of my time. He disapproves of badges and prizes, believing them to be divisive and elitist, breeding pride and envy. But then, life is like that. We are equal only in the sight of God.

Of course, ten years from now Jane and the two Emilys will grin, embarrassed if reminded of the little smocks festooned with badges which once they wore so proudly. But I dare to hope they will one day be sewing badges on their own children's sleeves and recapturing the dreams they thought they had lost in the high-tech rat-race of the twenty-first century.

Because even if everything is then on video-tape (perish the thought) and the only books are instruction manuals for electronic gadgets, there will still be dreams to share of love and excitement and wonder—dreams of the Kingdom we re-enter through the mind of a child.

Won't there?

Hidden Power

As soon as we sat down to breakfast on the hotel terrace overlooking the lake I knew it was going to be a magnificent day. I knew this because the top of my yogurt carton, instead of tearing messily, came off cleanly in one piece. Omens don't come any happier than that.

Carlo joined us for a final cup of coffee. A bright, smiling young man with all the spirited panache of the northern Italians. 'Va bene?' he said.

I nodded. 'Benissimo.' It was a day for superlatives.

'Buono. Today we go to Cascata del Toce. Is waterfall, no? In mountains. Very 'igh. You bring wellies.'

'Wellies?' Sheena said incredulously. Not a cloud in the sky, the lake like blue silk, the temperature up in the seventies and rising.

'Is very cold in mountains, signora. No wellies, you shiver.'

'Oh, *woollies*,' Sheena said, smiling.

'Si. Wellies. Keep you 'ot, no?'

I did not enjoy the first half hour of the journey. We took the main trunk road going north from Stresa and the traffic was formidable. Little Fiats slid recklessly in and out between enormous trucks which bore down on us with flashing lights and blaring horns. Fists were shaken through open sun roofs, compliments vigorously exchanged (I think they were compliments), sudden death courted. The Italians are a deeply religious people and it shows in their driving which is one part skill to three parts blind faith.

Sheena looked pointedly at Carlo's seat belt hanging unused on the door pillar behind him. 'In England,' she said with hardly a tremor in her voice, 'we always wear our seat belts. It's the law, you see.'

Carlo smiled approvingly, overtaking a truck with inches to spare. 'In Italy, too, signora.'

'But you're not wearing yours.'

Carlo shrugged, unperturbed. 'Que sera sera.'

What will be, will be. I wedged myself into the corner of the rear seat and closed my eyes, the promise of the yogurt carton suddenly fragile.

But when we turned off towards the mountains it was a different story. As the roar of the traffic faded away behind us, I opened my eyes to a wooded valley sleeping innocently in the morning sunlight. The empty road climbed steeply through a series of picture postcard villages where little white houses with painted shutters clustered on grassy terraces above the river. Flower baskets blazed with colour on the balconies. Old men in smocks and berets sat drinking grappa in tiny, open-fronted cafés. There were women washing clothes in communal stone troughs, Disney-type cows with long eyelashes and bells hung round their necks, children waving as we passed.

We stopped on a ridge between two valleys to take photographs. When Carlo switched off the engine the silence was as light and as warm as a cellular blanket. We found ourselves speaking in whispers. The air was vibrant with a kind of breathing beauty, the stillness of the trees almost eerie. It was as though we had slipped through a time warp back to the first day of Creation; to a green and golden Eden where only God had walked before us and the cunning serpent had yet to be born. 'Is nice, no?' Carlo said.

'Marvellous,' I said, lost in wonder. 'Meraviglioso.'

He smiled forgivingly. 'Meravigliosissimo, signor.'

As I said, it was a day for superlatives.

At the little albergo in the last village before the waterfall, we ate huge cheese rolls as big as small loaves and drank ice-cold lager while Carlo had a long, frenetic conversation with the innkeeper; a dignified figure who wore a white apron over his baggy blue trousers and whose serene eyes belied the ferocity of his black scimitar moustache. There was much gesticulation and the words tumbled out in torrents, both men speaking at the same time. Sheena and I ate unconcernedly. Italian conversations always sound like *Il Trovatore* without the music.

Eventually the innkeeper shrugged his shoulders up round his ears and spread his hands—bad news in any language. Carlo turned to us, his face clouded. 'I am much sorry, signore, signora. Today waterfall is chiuso.'

'Closed?' I said unbelievingly.

'Si. Is closed.'

We considered this incredible news for a moment or two. We had seen photographs of the waterfall; a great, white cascade falling hundreds of feet into the valley below. Thousands of gallons of water per minute foaming over the lip of the precipice. And it was closed?

'But that's ridiculous,' Sheena said. 'How can you close a waterfall?'

The answer was the hydro-electric station they had built at the head of the valley, diverting the water through massive pipes tunnelling deep into the mountain to drive the turbines. Only on Sundays was it allowed to follow its natural course and tumble in splendour over the precipice. And today was Monday.

I was beginning to go off yogurt in a big way.

Having come so far we went on up to the top. Stood in the thin mountain air (in our woollies) on the edge of the drop with the snow-clad peaks all around us and the crater lake which fed the waterfall black in the sunlight. Stood and looked wryly at the trickle of water spilling over and tried to visualize it in full spate. It was rather like arriving at Westminster Abbey the day after the Coronation. The surroundings were magnificent, a setting for glory. But the glory had departed.

Suddenly Carlo's eyes brightened. 'Is like chiesa, no?'

'The church?' I said, puzzled.

'Si, church.' He grinned slyly. 'Work only on Sunday. In week, closed.'

It was not a bad image (his imagination was better than his driving), upside-down but not inaccurate. On Sunday, church and waterfall were on display; all the splendour, all the grandeur. The river of Faith exulting for all to see and marvel at. But that was not work. That was celebration. The glorious liberty of the Spirit.

I thought of all that wild, white water harnessed to the turbines from Monday to Saturday, bringing warmth and light and power to the people in their homes. Unseen, unheard, taken for granted. But there. For the church as for the waterfall, the real work began when the Sunday display was over.

I grinned back at him, 'Yes, Carlo. Just like the church.'

AFRICA SINGS

The school was just one big room with mud-brick walls and a corrugated iron roof dented by the hail storms which sweep across the Northern Transvaal in the summer months. There was no glass in the windows. Only the Chief's house had glass windows. Everyone else in the village lived in thatched rondavels with no windows at all, just a low opening for the doorway and a hole in the roof to let out the smoke from the cooking fires. The rondavels clustered in little groups along the floor of the valley like giant beehives. There were clumps of aloes and a small lake sheltered by the hills and great splashes of yellow where the mealies (maize) grew. It was a place of quiet beauty and great poverty.

The village, like so many in the Transvaal, suffered from a generation gap. There were children and grandparents but no mothers or fathers. They were away working in Johannesburg, two hundred and fifty miles to the south, sending what little money they could spare to provide clothes for their children and enable the villagers to shop at the Indian store three miles away where the track joined the main road. The soil was thin and grey, heavily over-cropped, crying out for fertilizers. Without the money sent back from Johannesburg, the village would die.

The children sat facing us on long wooden benches, bare-legged, bare-footed, skimpily dressed, their black faces polished with smiles. They ranged in age from six to sixteen and had names like Bella and Plantina and Meeryjane (the girls) and Sixpence, September and Joshua (the boys). But they all had the same surname: Mamabola. Everybody in the village from the Chief down was a Mamabola, so they all called each other by their first names. It made for an easy, family atmosphere.

James and I sat in front of the blackboard on wooden kitchen chairs; the only chairs in the village outside the Chief's house. Country Africans are more comfortable sitting straight-legged on the floor.

Chueo, the young schoolmaster, stood beside us; a tall, lithe Zulu from Natal in a dark suit and a white shirt. He was a graduate of Fort Hare University and the chairs belonged to him. He was talking to the children in Bpedi—one of the most complex and difficult of African tribal languages. They listened to him attentively, their eyes fixed on him and occasionally turning to look at us. Especially at me.

'What's he saying?' I whispered in James's ear.

'He's introducing you, old son,' James said.

'Ah.' James had been coming up to the village every couple of months for the past six years, spending a day there, giving his personal support to Chueo, courteously complimenting the Chief on his village, showing interest and concern. Making them feel we cared.

Now I was taking over. In future I would be making the visit alone, representing my white congregation in Pretoria.

It was two o'clock in the afternoon. Under the iron roof of the school the air was still, oozing heat, heavy with the scent of woodsmoke from the cooking fires. Chueo had given us lunch, his wife killing a chicken and stewing it with herbs and mealies. We had eaten on the veranda of his house (a lean-to built on the end of the school wall) with the entire village sitting silently watching us. For most of the children we were the only white men they had ever seen.

The food lay comfortably in my stomach, the flow of incomprehensible Bpedi washed over me, my eyelids began to droop. Suddenly, Chueo switched to English. 'Today the two fathers have come to see us,' he said, using the polite African term for honoured guests. 'They have brought us gifts.' He pointed to the sack of sweets James always carried on these trips. 'I know you are all grateful to them.'

The children clapped, pink-palmed hands raised above their heads, eyes and teeth gleaming in their ebony faces. Chueo bowed to us with quiet dignity. 'We have little to give you in return except our thanks and the gift of a song.'

He signalled to the children to stand. There was no piano, no guitar, not even a tuning-fork. Chueo's finger pointed. Four children opened their mouths. A perfect four-note chord filled the room. They began to sing, moving to the rhythm of the music, swaying and bobbing in unison as their voices harmonized. The bare, brick box of a room opened like a flower as fifty voices swooped down upon us in a great, warm wave of sound that carried us away across the lake and over the mountains, up into the vast blue arch of the sky. I understood not one word of Bpedi but the meaning came through; all the tears, all the longing, the laughter, the love, the hope.

This was authentic, unspoiled singing. The voice of Africa. Not the shamed Africa of the squalid black townships festering in violence and bitter humiliation, but the free Africa of the high veld and the great rivers, the golden mealie fields, the little thatched rondavels under the black velvet of the night sky brilliant with stars. An Africa systematically robbed of its riches, starved of its plenty, its ancient traditions scorned and outraged. An Africa miraculously reborn with hope in each new generation.

When they had finished I felt the prickle of tears behind my eyelids, a lump in my throat, shamed by the beauty of the singing, grateful for its enduring strength.

Beside me, James stood up and smiled. 'Thank you,' he said. 'That was very nice.'

I looked at him with astonishment. Nice? That glorious river of music nice? Superb, yes. Magnificent. Moving. But—nice?

Worse was to come.

James said urbanely, 'Now I'm going to sing you a little song. An English song. And when my friend here comes again, perhaps you'll be able to sing it to him, eh?'

And he took a breath and began:

Jesus loves me, this I know
For the Bible tells me so...

After the subtle rhythms and inventive harmonies of the African song the simple little tune seemed woefully thin. An accomplished singer might have got away with it—just. But James, although he had a good speaking voice, was tone-deaf. He sang atrociously.

There was no applause when he sat down. African children are polite but also embarrassingly honest. On this occasion, honesty won.

Totally unaware of the gaffe he had committed, James smiled, unperturbed. 'A bit over their heads, I fancy,' he said quietly.

I gave him a wan smile.

Chueo's finger pointed at the children. Up came that lovely chord, hanging like a jewel in the still afternoon air. And then they were off. They took James's little tune and improvized on it for three minutes, tossing the melody from trebles to basses and then to the contraltos, weaving intricate patterns of harmony into it, giving it a heartbeat of driving, leaping rhythm.

It was a tour de force which would have brought the house down in the Albert Hall (and in La Scala at Milan, too). I sat entranced as they brought it to a roaring crescendo, held the final note impossibly long and true on a vibrant column of sound and cut it with precision. Shining eyes fixed on James, they stood sweating and smiling, breathless with pleasure.

James got up calmly. 'Yes,' he said with a forgiving smile. 'Well, of course, I don't expect you to get it right first time.'

When people talk about the problems of Africa I think of that moment long ago and the unbelieving disappointment in the children's faces as their smiles faded and their eyes took on that blank, shuttered look which is the African's defence against hurt.

James was a kindly man with love in his heart. But it is not enough just to love. There has also to be understanding, the ability to listen. And in Britain, as in Africa, that means being willing to recognize each other's special gifts, however strangely expressed. And to accept them with grace.

A Question of Trust

H ew gave me a pocket calculator this year for my birthday.

Unlike his sister and two brothers, all of whom are creators of dreams, Hew is a realist. He is also brilliant with figures, a gift he has inherited from my father who could add up three columns of pounds, shillings and pence simultaneously and with unbelievable speed, worked out percentages in his head and understood the dark mysteries of trigonometry. It is a gift which has passed me by without even a nod of recognition.

As a schoolboy I learned my tables by heart and can still recite them perfectly. Ask me what three sevens are and I answer 'twenty-one', quick as a whip, without conscious thought. But it is just a number. It doesn't mean anything. Ask me how much three pub sandwiches at 75p each cost and I need a pencil and paper and at least five minutes of absolute quiet. And still get it wrong.

When I was first introduced to algebra I experienced a false dawn of hope. The x's and y's (and the a's, b's and c's) were old friends well-met in a crowd of alien figures. Letters make words and words I understand. Alas, I discovered all too quickly that the letters in algebra had nothing whatever to do with words. They simply stood for unknown quantities which, so far as I was concerned, would forever remain unknown. It was my first experience of treachery. A moment of innocence lost.

I picked my way uneasily through the perils of lowest common denominators and highest common factors, fell into the twin pits of quadratic and simultaneous equations and clambered out into the sixth form in a cloud of unknowing. I could parse a sentence with nonchalant ease, conjugate the principal irregular Latin verbs (pluperfect and all) and distinguish instantly between a trochee and a dactyl. But only by a rare and happy accident could I hope to solve one of those extraordinary mathematical problems which required me to discover how long it would take three men with one-gallon buckets to fill a bath out of which the water was escaping down the plug-hole at the rate of six pints a minute. I felt then, as I do still, that if they'd had any sense at all they would have inserted the plug first and saved themselves (and me) a lot of hassle.

Mathematics in the sixth was taught by the headmaster (a Cambridge scholar of repute) who initiated us into the mystic rites of the slide-rule, that Machiavellian forerunner of the computer. I remember handling it with the clumsy reverence of total ignorance, sliding the little metal frame up and down at random like a beginner searching for the right note on a trombone. And, like a beginner, never finding it.

At the end of the term, the headmaster said, 'When we started this course I told you that a slide-rule always gives you two answers, one of which is manifestly absurd and should be disregarded.' His eyes met mine across the classroom with a look of wounded despair. 'I wish now to amend that statement,' he said with dangerous politeness. 'When Jackman uses a slide-rule *both* answers are manifestly absurd.' It was one of those truths which are self-evident, as my examination marks proved in due course. I didn't get any.

Emerging into the adult world with an education as lopsided as the Tower of Pisa, I learned to bluff my way through the hazards of bank statements and income tax returns, pretending an expertise I did not possess until I could afford to pay an accountant to do it for me. I became wary of promises like: 'Five per cent discount for cash,' for whilst I understand this means five pounds in a hundred, I always seem to be buying things priced at £41.36. What five per cent of that is, your guess is better than mine.

I also have difficulties with odd pennies. The man in front of me in the queue says helpfully, 'I've got the odd penny,' and puts it down triumphantly on the counter. His reward is a grateful smile from the shop assistant. All very pleasant and co-operative. My purchases come to £1.49. I repeat the magic phrase, proffering two pound coins and a penny, to receive a puzzled stare tinged with pity, reminiscent of my headmaster. The only consolation is that I always get my penny back, which is more than the man in front of me does.

When the children were younger we were hooked on Scrabble, a game of which I thoroughly approve and which I used to win with monotonous panache. Until Hew was old enough to join in.

He was, to begin with, an unimpressive player and no threat to me, being handicapped by a limited vocabulary derived very largely from comics. When I ruled that words like Wham, Zap and Kerplunk were not acceptable he was both incredulous and hurt. He also had a tendency to spell logically (with a d in the middle) rather than conventionally, which didn't help. But soon—all too soon—he began to win. Every time. When I put down a six letter word beginning with z (not easy) to collect 18 well-earned points he would add on an s and make it the first letter in a three-letter word cunningly sited to include a triple-letter square. This would give him a cool 50. I protested that playing by the figures, not the letters, was dead against the spirit of the game. Hew looked mildly surprised and referred me politely to the rule book which he had read more carefully than I. We don't play Scrabble much these days.

We do however have an occasional game of Monopoly, usually at Christmas when there is a deep reservoir of goodwill in the family. I can claim, with all due modesty, to be rather good at that, bankrupting everybody else to finish owning acres of property and more money than the bank. Hew says this is because I am an honest cheat; that is, one who doesn't realize he is cheating. I have a sneaking feeling he may be right. He usually is.

The calculator lies on my desk drinking in power from the morning sunlight (how, I don't begin to understand). No bigger than an ice-cream wafer, it can add, subtract, divide, multiply and work out percentages. It also has a memory which can be erased at the touch of a button (instant amnesia). If ever a man needed such a miracle of modern science I am he. I should be grateful and I am, of course. Only…

To be honest, I don't trust it, except to confirm what I already know. When it tells me 5 x 5 = 25 I happily agree. But I knew that anyway. But when I ask it to divide 48,736 by 29.5 (which it does with disdainful ease as if it knows I am merely testing it) I am unable to accept the result until I have worked it out for myself by long division (and divisions don't come any longer than mine)—three times, in fact, before I arrive at the same answer it produced in the twinkling of an eye.

Perhaps I am still mentally scarred by that traumatic encounter with a slide-rule. Or perhaps I am now too old a dog to learn new tricks. But I have learned at least one thing: far from being a substitute for faith, science depends upon it. If I am to benefit from this solar-powered miracle I'm going to have to believe it can do what the handbook says it can. And trust it to do it correctly, believing where I cannot prove.

And that is a salutary thought for a man who has spent more than forty years trying to persuade his congregations to do just that.

Is Anyone There?

Interesting the way people answer the telephone.

In Italy they are brisk and positive. Ring an Italian number and a voice says, 'Pronto' which means, 'I'm ready.' We British are more cautious. Ring an Englishman in his home and you get a tentative, 'Hullo?' Ring him at his office and he responds with an impatient, 'Yes?' implying that he has more important things to do than talk to you. Ring British Telecom and they play you something soothing by Vivaldi. Americans say, 'Who is this?' (inviting the answer, 'You, you fool') and New Zealanders invariably say, 'Are you there?' and seem agreeably surprised if you say you are.

I suppose it's because, even now, we still find it unnatural to talk to a disembodied voice. Unnatural and somehow intimidating. Conversations need facial expressions, gestures.

Without these aids to communication words become vulnerable to misinterpretation, silences intimidating (Have they hung up on me? Have I upset them?).

Difficult over the phone, it becomes positively dismaying over the radio where you talk and nobody ever answers...

'When you're ready, then,' the producer says, a variation on my New Zealand friends' approach which puts the ball unnervingly in my court.

I pick up my scripts and push open the heavily padded door which leads from the control room into the studio. As always, it is like walking through a hole in time. Functional, air-conditioned, acoustically dead, a broadcasting studio is the epitome of loneliness; a room with no memories of yesterday, no dreams of tomorrow. If there is a halfway house between this world and the next it will look and feel like this.

I sit down at the circular table in front of the microphone. Through the thick, plate-glass window in one wall I can see them talking and laughing in the world I have just left; the producer and his secretary, the studio manager, the technician. I can see them but I can't hear them. This accentuates the loneliness, the feeling of being in limbo.

The studio manager is young with cool, intelligent eyes. He smiles at me politely and flicks a switch on his console. His voice comes out of a speaker cabinet as big as a wardrobe. 'Comfortable?' he says gently, like a dentist unhooking his drill.

I nod tensely.

'So,' he says, 'what did you have for breakfast this morning?'

I reel off the sort of breakfast menu favoured by Edwardian gentlemen of leisure in country houses; porridge, haddock, kidneys on toast, bacon and eggs with sausages and croquette potatoes, kedgeree, toasted muffins, marmalade, coffee. He believes not one word of it, is interested only in monitoring my voice and achieving what he calls a level.

'That's fine,' he says. 'We'll go for a take, shall we? Green coming up in ten seconds.'

I clear my throat and wait. The big second hand on the studio clock jerks soundlessly round the dial. My script lies flat on the green baize, the pages unstapled now, unlikely to rustle. The trick is to make it sound unscripted; a spontaneous flow of words like one half of a conversation.

Suddenly the little green light in front of me glows. I begin to read. It is difficult to believe that anyone is listening—will be listening next week when the recording goes out on the air.

'Look at me when I'm talking to you,' my father used to say when I was a small boy. I realize now that it was not just a request for common courtesy. It was a plea for recognition, for response; the need to see his words reflected in my expression.

I stare at the microphone's blind head, willing it to grow eyes, a nose, a mouth—a face I can relate to, communicate with. Is this why people have always carved images of the gods to whom they pray? Because talking to an idol is better than talking to yourself?

I finish the first script and look up at the window. The producer, ever generous, puts up his thumbs and smiles. Through the speaker his voice says, 'I'll buy that, Stuart.'

I do three more scripts one after the other. They are designed to be slotted into someone else's live programme so timing is vital. Twelve seconds too short is as unprofessional as twelve too long. It is surprisingly hard work. I have been doing it for a number of years and it never gets easier. At the end of the session (eight scripts in all) I am sweating hard in spite of the air-conditioning, drained of nervous energy.

But then it is resurrection time. Out through the padded door into the land of the living. Smiles, voices coming directly out of people's mouths, coffee in paper cups. Everyone is pleasant and polite. The producer thanks me ('Another great set, old son'). I thank the studio manager. He thanks the producer's secretary. Everybody thanks the technician. The BBC is lubricated with coffee and gratitude. Only the technician stands aloof, accepting our thanks, giving none of her own.

She is young and thin, wearing jeans and a man's shirt flapping over her hips. She has carefully untidy hair and wears what seems to be heavy stage make-up. Her name is Fred. She is nineteen and different. She puts the reel of tape in its box, writes down the programme code number and looks at me with bored, black-rimmed eyes. 'What name was it again?' she says, as if I were already buried in an unmarked grave.

The producer's secretary (who is poised, chic and stunningly good-looking) shakes her head apologetically and tells her. Fred writes it down as Jackson, picks up the plastic Marks and Spencer carrier she uses as a handbag and bangs out into the corridor.

'Good at her job, hopeless with people,' the producer says, scratching out Jackson and writing in my name.

The following Wednesday morning I switch on my radio. The disc jockey fades out a track from Andrew Lloyd Webber's latest album and introduces me with a nicely-judged blend of serious bonhomie. At least, he gets my name right. And there I am, talking away to myself in that air-conditioned tomb under Broadcasting House.

Because I have sweated out the script on the typewriter, polished it, cut it down to size, polished it again and then read it against the clock in the studio, to me it sounds trite and stale. Who would want to listen to this pedestrian monologue? Who, listening, would find it of any value? I remember that there are seven more to come and mentally cringe.

But an hour later the phone rings. Somebody has taken the trouble to trace my number through Directory Enquiries. Somebody who really knows about loneliness. He talks quietly in an educated voice brittle with tears. After a hesitant start it all spills out in a torrent of words. The road accident which killed his wife and left him a nervous wreck, unable to work, unable to face the sympathy of neighbours, unable to forgive himself. Without a job he had to let his house go, move into a little private concentration camp of doubt and grief in a bed-sit. He says he thought God had forgotten him, the way all his friends seemed to have done. He says I'm the first person he has spoken to in more than a week.

The urgent, fragmented sentences tumble into my mind. The money worries, the scrappy meals, the endless, grinding loneliness of his life. Especially the loneliness.

Suddenly I realize he's not whining, not sorry for himself. He's excited. Grateful. Grateful for those banal words I churned out last week and he picked up on his transistor this morning. He talks about new hope, about the courage to begin again, about the sense of someone, somewhere, caring. And he says, 'Thank you. Thank you.'

I listen with a kind of shamed surprise that a handful of words dropped into the gap between two pop records should have reached a fellow human being in desperate need of reassurance. A lonely man who rings up out of the blue and tells me he's started to live again.

'It won't be easy,' he says. 'I know that. But nothing that's worthwhile ever is, is it?'

I remember the pages of my script spread out on the studio table, the bored eyes of the technician. 'No,' I say gently, 'it's never easy.'

'But possible.' He makes it half a statement, half a question. 'That's what you said. With God everything's possible.'

'You'd better believe it,' I say, as much to myself as to him.

BLITHE SPIRITS

I met my first eccentric when I was a student, nearly fifty years ago.

He was a Doctor of Divinity, tall and lean, with amused blue eyes, a thick thatch of white hair and the exquisite manners of an Eighteenth Century gentleman. Well into his sixties, he looked a distinguished fifty-five and he tried to teach me Hebrew, which he spoke with a lilting Scots accent (I had not previously visualized Moses in a kilt) and enviable fluency. I never got anywhere with that extraordinary intricate language. I was schooled in Latin and Greek and had a profound mistrust of a tongue in which no vowels are written down, only the consonants. But he taught me much else—about life and faith and laughter. He was as full of those things as a child; a restless, questing spirit energized by innocence and an unshakeable belief in his fellow men.

It was one of his pleasures to take his students for country drives in his ancient, stately car; an experience which was in itself a practical lesson in trust, for he was as unpredictable in his driving as in everything else. He was given to stopping without warning on the crest of a hill to admire the view. And to sitting through three changes of traffic lights whilst expounding some abstruse point of Hebrew grammar, oblivious to the horns hooting angrily behind him.

So it was that two of us were with him one fair April day, bowling along at a cracking pace with a fine disregard for the Highway Code, sitting in the back seat, knees drawn up, hands clasped white-knuckled, in that curious attitude of prayer which has been called: The Nonconformist Crouch.

Just before a left-hand bend, we came upon a roadside sign which urged us in large red letters, to PREPARE TO MEET THY GOD. As we came (miraculously) out of the bend, there was a tattered figure standing forlornly on the grass verge. Old clothes fastened with bits of string, broken boots, a straggling grey beard, deep-set eyes—the archetypal tramp. The Doctor braked hard, flung open the passenger door, inclined his head with grave courtesy and said, 'Get in, my dear Sir, get in. You're not a bit like I expected.'

Since then I have come across eccentrics around the world, always with pleasure, sometimes with a kind of awe.

Like the highly-educated (and utterly charming) lady who used to read Homer in the original Greek from a book clipped to the handle of her lawnmower as she cut the grass in her garden. She always went to the shops with two baskets. One on her left arm for the shopping, the other on her right to hold the wool she was knitting up as she walked. And, if the pattern was particularly complex, had been known to walk back without actually entering a shop.

Then there was Anne, small of stature, large of heart; a good friend and a superb pastry-cook. One afternoon she arrived on our doorstep with a white paper bag containing a dozen chocolate eclairs fresh from the oven. 'I won't come in,' she said politely, 'because if I do you'll only make tea and I shall eat most of these myself.'

That was in early July. Some eight weeks later, she came again with another paper bag in which there was a rather nice plate. Empty. 'I'm so sorry', she said with a radiant smile. 'Those eclairs I brought the other day. They should've been on this plate. Don't rush to return it. Any time you're passing will do.'

We waited a week (tactfully) and returned the plate.

'Goodness,' she said. 'Have you eaten them all already?'

There was no answer to that.

All eccentrics are remarkable but some are dauntingly so, being also people of high principles.

Oliver was one of these. He kept a bookshop in a small market town. The shop was sited on a corner with a view down the length of the High Street. Above the window, bright with multi-coloured dust jackets, was a high, white-painted wall which reflected the sunlight like a beacon, dominating the town. What the advertisers call a prime site. But Oliver reacted to advertisers—especially those who liked to put up big, brash posters on walls—much the way Don Quixote reacted to windmills. He didn't just dislike them. He hated them with a high and holy hatred splendid to behold. Unless you were on the receiving end.

Even more than posters, he hated those two life-sized wooden men who used to be seen frozen in mid-stride in a field, joined together by a ladder bearing the name of a paint manufacturer. As a young man, Oliver and a companion (who shared his views) spent weekends riding local trains, plotting those wooden men on an Ordnance Survey map and returning after dark on a motorbike to saw them down.

All this was unknown to the man from the advertising agency who walked into Oliver's shop one day. 'Good morning to you,' he said, his voice a velvet glove over the iron fist of his salesmanship. 'My name is Brown and I've come to put a bit of money your way.'

'Have you now?' Oliver said warily. Running a bookshop is not the easiest of ways to earn a living and he was no stranger to hard times.

'That wall above your window,' Brown said. 'I can use it. Wonderful position. Nobody can walk up the High Street without noticing it. Just what we're looking for.'

'To do what?' Oliver said.

Brown laughed. 'Rent it, of course. Put one of our biggest posters up there. An investment. Money in the bank. For you as well as us.'

'I'm sorry,' Oliver said. 'No.'

'Now let's not be too hasty,' Brown said, his smile hardening. A big, bluff, tweedy man, thick-skinned, good at his job. 'When I say money in the bank I'm not talking peanuts.'

'I didn't suppose you were,' Oliver said equably.

'No, I'm talking real money. Regular quarterly payments. Monthly if you prefer.'

Oliver shook his head. He had a rather good head; bright red hair, intelligent, deceptively mild eyes, an Elizabethan beard. 'Not interested, thank you.'

Brown grinned. 'You will be when I tell you how much.' He named a figure.

Oliver blinked. 'A quarter?'

'A month. And no outlay on your part. No upkeep costs either. We'll take over the exterior decoration of your shop at no cost to you.'

'No,' Oliver said.

'Not enough?' Brown raised his eyebrows. 'Right. We'll double it.'

'Not even if you trebled it,' Oliver said and politely opened the door.

A week later Brown was back, offering four times the

original rent. Oliver refused it without a moment's hesitation. And went on refusing as the weeks passed and the sum offered increased steadily.

The word got around that Oliver's wall was a gold mine and the town watched with amused awe. Rumour had it that Oliver would be far better off—several thousand pounds per annum better off—renting his wall than selling books. Could afford to retire, in fact.

His bank manager had a tactful little chat with him, hinting that a regular income would be appreciated at the bank's end.

'At my end, too,' Oliver said. 'But not from a poster on my wall.'

'Advertising's a fact of life, I'm afraid,' the bank manager said.

'A fact of your life, perhaps, but not of mine,' said Oliver who refused to travel by the London Underground because the walls of the stations were defaced with posters.

Brown's final offer was to be the clincher. He walked into the shop, oozing a heady mixture of confidence and generosity, opened his cheque book and put it on Oliver's desk. The cheque was already made out to Oliver dated and signed. Only the amount was missing. Brown took out his pen. 'Put in as much as you want.' He unfolded a sheet of paper and laid it beside the cheque book. 'And sign on the dotted line.' It was a three-year contract with an option to renew.

Oliver smiled, perhaps a touch wistfully. As I said, there are easier ways to make a living than selling books. 'Full marks for trying. But the answer's still no. You're not going to vulgarize my wall.'

Brown stared at him. 'You don't approve of our product?'

'I use it regularly.'

'So, what's the problem?' Brown tapped the cheque book. 'I'm serious, you know. There's no catch. You can name your own price.'

'I haven't got a price,' Oliver said. 'It's a matter of principle and principles can't be bought.'

People said he was mad, of course. A bit touched. Perhaps he was. Touched with magic.

There is an old superstition that eccentrics are touched by God; that at birth a celestial finger is laid lightly on their heads or hearts—or perhaps both. They are chosen by their Creator to be that little bit different from the rest of us, that little bit more aware of values higher and deeper than most of us dare to believe in. It's as though they order their lives by a logic beyond our understanding; some sense of the extraordinary in the ordinariness of life. These adventurous spirits are special, set among us to remind us that things are not always what they seem. That life is not something we have invented and are able to control, but a gift of God to be respected and seized with joy.

They make us feel slightly uneasy and we laugh about them. But they have the magic; a blank cheque on the bounty of God.

Which is why we would be the poorer without them.

Easter Eggs

HONEST DOUBT

Every Easter Day when I was young there was a large chocolate egg wrapped in silver paper beside my plate on the breakfast table (and a clutch of smaller ones from aunts and uncles on the sideboard). My mother wore a new hat to church, my father sported a flower in his coat and I had new shoes or a pair of new gloves. There were no cards on the mantelpiece (cards were for Christmas and birthdays then), but a huge vase of flowers—usually daffodils— graced the hall table and the church was white with lilies. And for tea there was always fresh salmon and lettuce from the garden, peppery watercress, rhubarb and custard and an iced cake. Such little things to mark so great an occasion. But they live in my memory as the tokens of faith fulfilled.

People knew about Easter in those days. They didn't all believe what it was saying but they respected it and cherished the hope that it might be true. To translate hope into belief is not an easy thing to do, as Thomas the Doubter discovered. *Unless I see him, touch his wounds with my finger, hear him speak—I can't believe he's alive again.* Evidence, you see. That's what Thomas wanted, what we all want. To see, to hear, to touch. But we come too late in time to do that. All we have is the record left by those who were there that first Easter morning. The privileged few to whom he showed himself alive.

Like Mary of Magdala who loved him beyond all telling.

She was the first to see him. Weeping in the garden outside the empty tomb, the jar of embalming spices a mockery in her hands, she saw him through a mist of tears. She thought he was the gardener. What else was she to think? She had watched him die on Friday afternoon, helped to give him a hasty burial before the sun set and the Passover began, stood white-faced and trembling with shock as the great stone sealed the tomb and the guard was mounted. How could he be standing beside her now? But he was and when he spoke her name in that well-remembered voice she had thought silenced for ever, she blinked away her tears and saw him clearly.

Imagination? An hysterical woman tricked by grief into seeing the man she most wanted to see, had never expected to see again? The others thought so. Peter and John and the rest of them, sitting despondently in the house, facing another day of disillusion and heartbreak, a sleepless night behind them. Dreamers of a glorious dream which had died so cruelly on Skull Hill and left them lost and helpless. When Mary came bursting into the room, breathless with excitement, the words tumbling out of her mouth they didn't believe her. 'It seemed to us,' they wrote later, 'to be an idle tale.'

That is a confession which gives me hope. The sort of natural reaction we can understand and share. These were men who knew him intimately, who had left their homes and jobs to tramp the roads with him, dependent upon charity for food and shelter. They had seen him hold great crowds spell-bound, outwit his enemies with a casual word, speak to little children with love and laughter. Seen him set people free from illness and suffering, demonstrating at weddings and funerals the reality of the Kingdom which is God's gift to mankind. If anyone should have believed he was risen from the dead it was these men. Indeed, he had promised them he would rise and they knew from experience that he unfailingly kept his promises.

You would think they would not only have believed Mary but would have proudly set their belief down in writing. A resurrection was exactly what they needed, the way a man setting up in business needs capital he can draw on. There were only eleven of them; insignificant men of no social standing—fishermen, tax-collectors, market gardeners, tradesmen. An unlikely company to be entrusted with changing the course of human history. They needed every bit of help they could get for so mammoth a task. What they didn't need was an admission of their own disbelief. But they made that admission and preserved it in writing. Told it not the way it should have been but the way it was. Hardly a prudent thing to do but at least honest. And that is the best of beginnings, as Thomas was to prove.

Later that afternoon, of course, it was different. By then the empty tomb was common knowledge in the city and the rumours rife. The High Priest was bribing the guards who had fled in terror from the open tomb to spread the word that the friends of Jesus had stolen his body and hidden it. In the Residency, Pilate, the Governor General who had reluctantly signed the death warrant, was miserably contemplating the ruin of his career. In the back-street house loaned to them by sympathizers, the eleven men had locked themselves away and were listlessly picking at their supper, wishing the rumours were true, needing tangible proof.

Suddenly he was there with them; a free spirit no walls or locked doors could confine. And that's what they thought he was—a spirit, a ghost. But the wounds were there in his hands and feet, identity marks they could not dismiss. Confused and afraid, they watched him helping himself to the food they were eating, smiling appreciatively, enjoying it. They knew then who he was and what he had done. Ghosts don't eat supper. Only a living, breathing man can do that.

And so they wrote it for us to read and ponder. A statement of faith founded on fact all the more convincing because of their earlier confession of doubt. If they were honest about that—and they were—can we doubt the honesty of that subsequent moment of joyful recognition? Remember, these men were to go to prison for their faith, some of them to the Roman gallows, some to death by stoning. You don't do that for a myth, nor for the ghost of what might have been. It takes courage and faith. Faith in the evidence of your own eyes. Faith in a living, risen man who called them his friends and whom they called God.

Let Thomas have the last word. Thomas called the Twin, not because he looked like Jesus but because he too was a carpenter. He had not been there at the supper in the shuttered house that first Easter Day and he doggedly refused to believe until he had seen for himself. But he was with them later in the week when it all happened again. Jesus suddenly in the room with them, greeting them cordially, looking at Thomas with a quizzical smile. 'Well then, Thomas,' he said. 'You wanted proof and proof you shall have. Come and touch my wounds. Don't be afraid. Satisfy yourself it really is I.'

And Thomas was on his knees, tears of joy and shame running down his face. 'My Lord,' he said simply, 'and my God.'

Of all those friends of Jesus, Thomas is the one we can most easily identify with. The man who discovered that faith is born of honest doubt, as the true life of the Kingdom is born out of death.

Enjoy your chocolate eggs, the Easter flowers, the cards. Behind these simple pleasures lies the secret of life for us all, made known in One who lived and died and rose again.

Happy Easter.

NEW EVERY MORNING

'Easter in March,' Henry said (you remember Henry?). 'Where's the sense in that?'

'It falls right at the end of March,' I said reasonably. 'On the day that British summertime officially begins, actually.'

'Summertime be blowed,' Henry said (or words to that effect). 'It's more like t'middle of winter is March.' He shook his head gloomily, 'It's t'brides as I feel sorry for. Standing about in draughty churchyards, shivering in thin frocks while the photographer fiddles wi' his tripod and light meter. I mean ter say, who wants to go on a honeymoon with a cold in t'head?'

He blew his nose defiantly. 'Nay, lad, it's right daft. I reckon as they ought to make it t'third Sunday in April every year. A fixed date same as for Christmas. Folk'd know where they were then.'

It was a typical Henry comment, dogmatic, practical, full of honest-to-goodness Yorkshire common sense. But I don't know…

I remember a far off, exciting Easter fifty odd years ago, coming down off the high desert country in west Iraq with a convoy of trucks into the upper Jordan valley and seeing grass for the first time in two years. New grass spread like a green velvet cloak over the hills above Galilee, bright with the startling reds and purples of millions of spring flowers. And the blue water of the lake mirroring the sky and the air delicious with the scent of orange blossom. A promised land indeed.

A couple of fishing boats were drawn up on the beach near Capernaum, the crews eating breakfast round a small fire of driftwood on the sand. They waved to us as we rolled past; big men, muscular, lean, burned by the sun and the wind, their dark eyes smiling. It was not hard to visualize among them a young Carpenter newly sprung to life, his troubles behind him, the whole waking world at his wounded feet.

It's a scene I have recreated in my mind each year on Easter Day in many different places. Each year the same, each year astonishingly fresh and new.

April in Devon, the fields along the Taw valley thick with wild daffodils. So thick that half a dozen of us spent most of Saturday afternoon picking great armfuls of them, choosing the best, wading knee-deep through a lake of yellow gold. And in the early evening, as we climbed over the stile to walk back to the station burdened with beauty, the fields behind us looked as full of flowers as if we had never been there. Perhaps they grow as prodigally in the Lake District. But I never fully believed Wordsworth's 'ten thousand saw I at a glance' until I went to Devon.

We took them to the church and stood them in white enamel pails of water down the aisle at the end of every pew, filled vases for every window ledge, arranged them in great, golden drifts around the communion table. And the next morning when we opened the church doors for Easter Day it was like walking into Paradise; possible to believe, in that moment of breath-taking loveliness that he was risen indeed.

When I said as much to Henry, he nodded. 'Right enough. April flowers and Easter go together. You can't have one without t'other.'

But you can.

Living and working in New Zealand, I had to come to terms with Christmas in mid-summer and Easter in late autumn. It had been the same in South Africa, of course. But Africa is full of sunlight and colour even in the winter. New Zealand isn't.

'Spring has now unwrapped the flowers,' sang the children in Auckland on Easter morning. But the spring was half a year away and the city gutters were choked with wet leaves as rain swept in cold from the Pacific. The imagery, magnificently right in Israel and England, was hopelessly wrong; not an aid to faith but a mockery of it.

Harvest Festival in the middle of Lent had been difficult enough; the richness of the land guiltily opulent in a season of austerity and fasting. But Easter on the threshold of winter was impossible; singing of new life in a dying season. What we needed was a new image of resurrection. A New Zealand image.

I found it on holiday in Gisborne.

Gisborne is a small town south of Auckland on the east coast of North Island. A pleasant, rather sleepy place with a superb beach and friendly people. Ideal for a quiet holiday but unremarkable. Except for one thing.

There is a headland above the beach, with grass and trees and a magnificent view along the coast. Pretty spot for a picnic, you might think. But also unique, not only in New Zealand but also in the world. Because of the positioning of the International Date Line, that headland in Gisborne is the first piece of dry land in the world on which the rising sun shines every morning at dawn.

'We get it first,' the Gisborne people say proudly. 'Never mind we're only a small town most people have never heard of. Every morning we get first go at the new day.'

'Aye, mebbe,' Henry said, carefully unimpressed. 'So what?'

'Ever heard of Eostre?' I said, just a touch smugly. I don't often get the chance to tell Henry something he doesn't know.

'Who's he when he's at home?'

'She,' I said. 'She was the ancient pagan goddess of the dawn. Gave her name to our Easter festival.'

'Ah,' Henry said. 'The sun also rises, eh?' He's like that, Henry. Quick to make the connection between the rising sun and the risen Son. Quite fond of quoting Hemingway, too. Well-read, you see.

I nodded. 'Every day, even in winter, the sun rises. We don't have to wait for spring to remind us of that. The imagery of Easter is up there for us to see, new every morning.'

How could it be otherwise? The Child born in the manger, imprisoned for thirty-three years in a human body, a captive of time and place as we all are, breaks out into freedom on Easter Day. A free spirit, alive not just in one body but in everybody, as comfortably at home in the New Zealand autumn as he is in the English spring.

A spirit like that—you can't pin him down to a particular day in a particular place. He is the ultimate expression of life; and the essence of life is movement. What else can we do but give him a movable feast?

'Happen you're right,' Henry said, a Christian at heart but shy with it. 'But I still think as we'd be better off having it on t'third Sunday in April.'

I must remember to send him an Easter egg on March 30th. And another one, just to show there's no ill-feeling, on April 20th.

EASTER JOURNEY

I left college in 1941 to join the RAF. Two weeks into the autumn term, it was, and I was halfway through my training. My New Testament tutor was not pleased.

'Does this mean you won't be giving me that essay on the Synoptic Gospels you owe me?' he said affrontedly.

I said I was afraid it did.

'Oh, dear.' He was a brilliant scholar living happily in the First Century AD, vaguely aware there was a war on, totally disinterested in it. 'In that case, I strongly advise you to insist on being sent to Palestine without delay. Then, perhaps, this unfortunate break in your studies—which you can ill-afford—will not prove to be a complete waste of time.'

As it turned out, he was right.

Three years later (the RAF had other plans for me before that) I arrived in Egypt by way of India, Persia and Iraq, put in for seven days' leave, hitch-hiked back across Sinai and booked into a Services club in Jerusalem. That evening I planned my pilgrimage.

Bethlehem first, of course, where it had all begun. The market square where Joseph and Mary had been turned away from the inn; the stepped street down which the shepherds had stumbled in a fever of excitement; the Church of the Nativity where armoured crusader knights had knelt stiffly to pray. Climbing to the tilted fields above the little town, I was aware of a sense of peace. And of expectancy. As if, when darkness came down the sky and the stars shone brightly, the ears of faith might still catch an echo of the angels' song. So small a place for so world-shaking an event.

To Nazareth next, by local bus full of country wives, hens pecking under the seats, two goats tethered insecurely on the roof, everyone eating garlic rings for breakfast. A pungent bouquet of smells.

Sitting on the old caravan route from Basra to Cairo, Nazareth was noisy. A bustling, brawling town of traffic jams and flies and acrid exhaust fumes. The hymn writer, secure in his Victorian vicarage, was right about the fair green hills but not about the turmoil in the streets. I changed buses for Tiberias and found tranquility. The great lake placid in the sunlight, the sloping fields bright with wild flowers, tree-shaded houses, the scent of orange blossom, a timeless beauty. Here, the off-duty legions had come to swim and laze in the summer heat, dreaming of home. And here the young carpenter had found his friends among fishermen, freedom fighters and tax collectors, firing their imaginations with a greater dream—the dream of the Kingdom, our ultimate home.

I spent a morning sailing in a Galilean fishing boat, the skipper a latter-day Simon Peter, bearded and big-fisted. A picnic on the beach, the morning's catch grilling over a small fire of driftwood, the round, flat loaves of bread broken and shared in friendship.

Sunrise the next morning. Mount Hermon floating in the sky, deceptively close across the water. *If you had faith the size of a mustard seed you could move mountains.* The challenge of that voice was everywhere; in the murmur of small waves lapping the beach, the whisper of the wind in the tall cypresses. In every shadow, round every corner, I expected to meet him—and perhaps did in the faces of farmers and boat builders and black-hatted rabbis.

After breakfast on Thursday I got a lift into Cana on a market truck. The Arab driver had the face of a hawk and the manners of a dove. He dropped me off outside an inn and I sat on the vine-covered veranda, drinking a belated toast to the happy couple whose wedding feast so long ago had been rescued from disaster when the wine ran out by a local boy destined for greatness. In the little school across the street the children were singing their ancient Jewish songs, as perhaps they had been singing then. Those had been the good days and golden, his enemies discomfited by his wit and learning, the hearts of the common people open to him, days of miracle and healing when it had seemed that nothing could stop him. Before the traps were set, the hostile witnesses rehearsed, the first faint shadow of the cross falling across his path.

The southbound Jerusalem bus took me back across Esdraelon past the Mount of Transfiguration rising tall out of the plain. There, one far, uncanny day, eternity had broken through the wall of time and three men, separated by centuries, had talked together as friends in a shaft of light whiter than a furnace flame. In that moment, heaven and earth were one and the dazed disciples saw him at last for who he truly was—not a carpenter with astonishing powers, but God.

The broad Galilean accents of my fellow passengers echoed that voice which had drawn the crowds like the magnet of God, proclaiming a Kingdom of peace and love not of this world. And I was suddenly one with that little band of men who had taken this road with him, three marvellous years behind them, the final triumph ahead.

The sun was setting as we came to Jerusalem. I got off the bus at the Jaffa Gate to walk up through the old city, my head filled with memories. Somewhere in those narrow streets was the house with the upper room where they had sat down to supper with him for the last time, a close-knit brotherhood, Judas still their trusted friend.

I crossed the site of the Antonia Fortress where the execution squad had mustered, taunting their prisoner with cruel jests. *Hail to you, King of the Jews.* I went out through the Zion Gate, scene of the short-lived ecstasy of Palm Sunday. Across the steep ravine Gethsemane was waiting. The shadows were thick under the twisted olive trees, the wind chill in the gathering dark. I turned and saw the city silhouetted against the first stars, felt its brooding menace and shivered. Was this how he had seen it on that night of betrayal, through tears of disappointment and despair while his friends slept uneasily on the grass? *Ah, Jerusalem, Jerusalem. You who kill the prophets…*

Easter was still three weeks away and Friday just another Friday. But not for me. I walked down the Via Dolorosa where he had staggered under the weight of the cross, his back shredded and bloody from the scourge; out through the Damascus Gate and up Skull Hill to stand on its scarred and barren crest. There were no coach parties of tourists in those war years, no importunate guides selling macabre souvenirs. But that squat, ugly hill outside the city wall was peopled with ghosts. I felt them clustering round me; the jeering sceptics mockingly urging him to come down from the cross and save himself, the weeping women, the bored, impassive soldiers who had seen it all before. The centuries telescoped in my mind. I heard the bone-crunching thud of the cross dropping into its socket, the rattle of dice as the soldiers gambled for his clothes, the sigh like the end of the world as the spear was thrust home and the cross came down and the Sabbath prayers began.

It is finished. I heard the words with understanding for the first time. Three years of vivid life, striding the country from Galilee to Jericho, the good news of God's love running like wildfire through the cottages of the poor, the rich men's villas. Blind eyes opened, crippled legs straightened, banished lepers welcomed back into their families. All the great speeches, the haunting stories, the wonder, the awe, the splendour—all this was ended in the space of a few traumatic hours. The impossible dream, which has haunted mankind since time began and which had seemed, for a little while, to be within our reach, crushed and scattered like dust in the wind.

I knew in that moment that the real horror of Good Friday lies not in the physical brutality of the Crucifixion—terrible as that was—but in the agony of the mind, the desolation of the spirit, the ultimate tragedy of man separated from his Maker. *My God, why have you forsaken me?*

What can we do in the face of such suffering and waste? We who four short months ago were rejoicing in the birth of Mary's little son. What can we do but weep for him—and for ourselves?

Early on Sunday morning, the last day of my leave, I went to the Garden Tomb. They say it is not the actual tomb which Joseph of Arimathea gave in an act of faith; not the actual place where the body of Jesus was laid to rest. No matter. It is, at least, the sort of tomb a rich man would have prepared for himself.

It was just as the Gospels describe it. A green place of beauty and peace, the garden shaded and cool, the tomb itself empty, the great round stone rolled back along its groove, a shaft of sunlight piercing the inner gloom. *He is not here. He is risen.*

If we think of Jesus as being a good man (and even non-Christians admit that much), the story ends on Good Friday. Dead men, however virtuous, do not come back from the grave. Only God can do that. God in human form, disguised as a village carpenter. *And the Word was made flesh and dwelt among us.* If we believe that at Christmas, why not at Easter?

Standing in that garden, I realized that the Resurrection, far from being a bit of wishful thinking tacked unconvincingly on to an appalling tragedy, is the only thing that makes sense—not only of the life and teaching of Jesus of Nazareth but of life itself. If death is the end of our story then that story is meaningless. A denial of the dignity of men and women, of the promise implicit in the birth of every child. A cruel joke at our expense. But if death is not the end but a new beginning, not a denial but a fulfilment, then there is hope for us all. And Easter is the promise of Christmas faithfully kept. *I am come that they might have life...*

'You've grown up while you've been away, my boy,' my New Testament tutor said, welcoming me back to college in 1946.

I smiled, remembering my pilgrimage. 'Yes, sir,' I said. 'You could say that.'

THE TRUE GLORY

He is nobody. He is everybody. We see him every night on 'News at Ten'; yesterday in Moscow, today in Belfast, tomorrow in Soweto or Kuwait or Bosnia. Wherever there is a crisis, he is there. A face in the crowd, glimpsed for a moment and then forgotten. The face of the man in the street, unknown, unremarkable, always there.

One April Sunday afternoon some two thousand years ago, he slipped out of Jerusalem to walk home to his village a few miles away. For once, he had a name. Cleopas. There was another man with him that day; his brother, perhaps, or brother-in-law, not important enough to be named. Cleopas and friend, then, caught up in a crisis of monumental significance. A matter of life and death, you might say.

It was a crisis they had been expecting; indeed, had been looking forward to. On the previous Friday morning, filled with hope, they had joined the thousands of pilgrims flocking into the city for the Passover, the big event of the Jewish year commemorating the great exodus from Egypt thirteen hundred years before, when Moses had led the people out of slavery, across the desert to the freedom of the Promised Land. But for Cleopas that year it was more than a feast of remembrance. His was a nation living under the iron heel of a Roman Army of Occupation, struggling to maintain its identity, sustained by a vision of deliverance in which Messiah would come to set his people free. Every year he went up for the Passover hoping to see Messiah's coronation and the end of all their troubles. And every year he went back home disappointed, telling himself, 'Next year in Jerusalem.'

He had been doing this all his life, but never more hopefully than this time. All the signs were there now, all the prophecies fulfilled in one man; a young carpenter from Nazareth. Jesus, the Deliverer. Jesus who, for three years of mounting excitement, had been stumping the country performing miracles of healing, drawing the crowds with astonishing speeches, delighting them with deceptively simple stories everyone could relate to, full of familiar details of their working lives, each one with a twist in the tail which set his listeners laughing and weeping—and thinking. The religious authorities in Jerusalem found these stories alarming, sometimes blasphemous, often treasonable. They seeded the crowds with their spies, watching, listening, asking sly questions to trap him; questions he skilfully turned back against them to the applause of the people. A series of bravura performances, witty, scathing and dangerous.

In two years he had built up a huge following with supporters in every section of society from scholars to illiterates, rich men to families on the breadline, and as the third year began a great wave of expectancy swept the country; a growing conviction that this, at last, was truly Messiah, ready now to declare himself. To the Romans, cynical, hard-headed soldiers and politicians, he was no more than a village carpenter overdosed on religion. A nuisance, perhaps, but not a serious threat. To the religious hierarchy he was a rabble-rouser to be watched and, if necessary, silenced. But to the ordinary people he was God's own son, promised, longed for through the bitter centuries of oppression, poised now to come into his Kingdom. This year in Jerusalem...

Cleopas and his companion went to the city that Friday morning dressed for a coronation, walking light-footed up the long road to Jerusalem, intent on getting good places in the Temple where Messiah would be crowned. As they topped the last rise they saw the city spread out before them in the sunlight, heard the roar of the crowds in the streets, saw the great Damascus Gate swing open and the procession come through. And it was a kind of coronation. But a dreadful parody of what they had come to see. For the crown was made of cruel thorns and the throne was a Roman gallows. Shocked and incredulous, they watched him die.

By the time the Passover Sabbath started at sunset, they had pieced together the details of his downfall. The treachery of Judas in Gethsemane, the mockery of a trial which condemned him in the teeth of the evidence, the Governor General signing the death warrant reluctantly and washing his hands of the whole tragic affair, the helplessness of the disciples, the fickleness of the crowds shouting him to his death. They stood in the Temple and watched the High Priest at the altar rehearsing that exodus under Moses, the solemn words brittle with self-righteous pride. Watched silently through their tears and went disconsolately to bed.

Passover Saturday was always a day for rejoicing, the holiday crowds thronging the streets with singing and laughter. But for Cleopas and all those like him who had pinned their faith on Jesus of Nazareth, it was a day of mourning and despair. A dream had died on Friday, lay cold in the tomb, the healing hands stilled, the golden voice silenced.

Numb with grief, Cleopas wakened early on Sunday morning to a rumour. Some women, arriving at the tomb to complete the time-honoured burial rites, had found it open and empty. One of them—Mary of Magdala who had been very close to Jesus—came running back to the house, breathless and bright-eyed with excitement, and said she had seen him, talked to him, touched him. 'He's not dead,' she said. 'He's alive. Alive.'

Nobody believed her. They put it down to hysteria, delayed shock, imagination triggered by overwhelming grief. Understandable. But obviously nonsense. Peter and John, clutching at straws, hoping against hope, went to investigate for themselves and found the tomb empty, as she had said. But there was no sign of Jesus. The general feeling was that the tomb had been broken open and robbed.

Cleopas and his friend lingered through the morning and into the afternoon, wanting to believe Mary, unable to convince themselves that it was true, hoping there would be more news. But there was none. No more sightings, no more encounters with a dead man come back to life. Only rumours spreading like wildfire through the city, disturbing the crowds, alerting the authorities. Finally, heavy-hearted, their world in ruins, the two of them decided to go home. They were halfway there when a stranger caught up with them.

'Hullo,' he said politely. 'Had a good Passover?'

The tactlessness of the remark stopped Cleopas in his tracks, 'You haven't heard what's happened this weekend?'

'What has happened?' the stranger said.

It all came pouring out then. Jesus of Nazareth, the things he said, the miracles, the promises, the hope they had had for him. 'We thought he was Messiah come at last,' Cleopas said. 'Were sure of it, in fact. Until last Friday when they—when they killed him.' His voice broke on the words.

'He's dead, then?' the stranger said calmly.

'Yes. At least...' Cleopas hesitated. 'We saw him die. The whole city saw him die...'

'But?'

Cleopas shook his head, 'Now there's a rumour that he—that he's alive again.' And he told the stranger of the empty tomb and Mary of Magdala's euphoria and the tense atmosphere in the city. 'But how can a dead man come back to life after three days?'

'You don't believe it?'

'I don't know what to believe,' Cleopas said bitterly. 'And that's the truth.'

'Truth?' the stranger said. 'Oh well, if we're going to talk about the truth...' He smiled. 'Let's walk on, shall we?' And he began to talk about Messiah, quoting the writings of the prophets, building up a logical pattern, opening their eyes to truths they had been taught in childhood but had never really understood. And as he talked the familiar words took on new meaning; all the questions answered, all the doubts removed.

Spellbound by his voice, conscious of a new flicker of hope, they soon found themselves in the village, the sun low on the horizon. When they stopped outside the house, the stranger said, 'I'll say goodbye, then.'

Cleopas hesitated, unwilling to let him go. There was something about him; something familiar yet different. 'It's getting late,' he said. 'Come in and eat with us. You'll be very welcome.'

'Well, thank you, Cleopas.'

My name, Cleopas thought. He knows my name. How?

'If you're sure it'll be all right?' the stranger said.

Sure? Cleopas thought wryly. I feel as though I'll never be sure of anything again as long as I live.

His wife had the table set for supper. They gave the stranger the place of honour and invited him to say Grace. He spoke the ancient Jewish words of thanksgiving, picked up the loaf, broke a piece off it and handed it round in the traditional way. And all at once the house was filled with light as if the sun had reversed its course and risen again. And the stranger was a stranger no longer.

'Well, Cleopas?' Jesus of Nazareth said. 'Do you still think it's nothing more than a rumour?'

And before they could speak, he was gone. There one moment, radiantly alive. The next, vanished.

The two men looked at each other in astonished relief not unmixed with shame. 'We ought to have known,' Cleopas said. 'When he was talking to us on the road. The way he explained things. We ought to have recognized him then.' He shook his head in happy wonder. 'Messiah in my house, breaking bread with us as... A couple of nobodies and he takes the trouble to sort out our problems and honour us with his company at supper. And out there the whole world is waiting for him.' He pushed back his chair and stood up in a fever of excitement. 'Come on, we've got to get back to Jerusalem and tell the others.'

'At this time of night?' his wife said. 'It's too late to be walking.'

'No,' Cleopas said. 'Not too late. We thought it was. Thought it was all over and finished. But it's only just beginning.'

First Mary of Magdala, then Cleopas and his friend. A broken-hearted woman seeing a vision? Two disappointed men hallucinating; hearing and seeing him because they wanted desperately for him to be alive? A great many people thought so then. And still do. Decent people, kindly, honest, worried about their children in an increasingly violent world. It's all there, all the evidence, all the post-Resurrection appearances in Jerusalem and Galilee. Impressive, moving, the fulfilment of all our dreams of a better world than this. But not easy to accept.

Until, that is, I turn back to Cleopas, little Mr Nobody entertaining God in his house. For the Easter miracle comes to me, as it did to him, in the simple things of daily life—companionship offered on a journey, hospitality provided for friend and stranger. Jesus of Nazareth came into this world as the child of an ordinary couple. He performed his miracles for ordinary people, listened to their hopes, calmed their fears. How else would he come back, except to such as us?

We don't know what happened to Cleopas. In the ensuing struggle to establish the Church there were martyrs and heroes and saints. He was never one of those, never famous, never a leader. And yet he endures; the man in the street, the representative of us all.

A curious name, Cleopas. Until you remember what it means. Cleopas—the true glory. Not the glory of man but of God in man. That was always Jesus' way. To walk past the self-important and the proud and touch the nobodies with splendour.

It still is.

Full Circle

ALL YOU NEED IS LOVE

D rew was ten, coming up to eleven, and for a long as he could remember George had been there, massive, gentle, infinitely obliging. A sort of heavy-breathing, canine Pooh to his Christopher Robin. Now he was no more, Sheena and I were sad. But Drew wept. For George, for his lost childhood, for all that now could never be. We would find him in the kitchen, standing by the window, George's thick leather leash in his hands, his eyes dark with memories. Catch him looking enviously at people with dogs in the park. Hear the muffled sound of sobbing through his bedroom door.

There was only one cure.

We waited a decent interval and then, ten days before Drew's birthday, rang up the kennel and got a shock. In the years during which we had enjoyed the pleasure of

George's company (and protection) the price of puppies had gone through the roof. We would need a second mortgage now to finance the purchase of another bulldog.

'There are other breeds,' Sheena said reasonably. 'Smaller. Easier to manage.'

I knew what she meant. We hadn't managed George. He had managed us. Patiently, firmly, without fuss, like an old family retainer.

I rang another dealer. He said he could do me a very fair Sealyham pup for fifty pounds. In the world of dogs, small may be beautiful. Cheap it isn't.

'I'm not looking for a show dog,' I said. 'Just a pet for...'

'Show dog?' He made a strangled noise over the phone. 'A show dog would set you back three times that amount, sir.'

'You've nothing under fifty?'

I heard him sniff. 'Got a miniature dachs. Of a sort. Short-backed, a bit too long in the leg. Let you have him for thirty-five.'

But somehow I didn't fancy a long-legged dachs. Not after George.

A friend who kept two Siamese cats (but was otherwise quite normal) suggested the RSPCA but I shook my head. 'Not a mongrel. I like a dog to look like a dog, not a mobile hearth rug.'

He grinned. 'They're not all mongrels, y'know. Go down to the kennels and have a look. The trick is to decide what you want before you go. Then keep a cool head and a moderately hard heart.'

We sat down and thought about it. Sheena even made a list. Short-coated, so it wouldn't moult all over the sitting-room carpet. A year to eighteen months, which would solve the problem of house-training (George as a puppy had been anxious to please—occasionally too anxious). Smallish, so it wouldn't eat too much. Female, because (she said) they are more home-loving. I pointed out that nobody could be more masculine than George had been and he had loved his home so much that only on exceptionally fine days could he be persuaded to walk further than the front gate and back. And that very slowly.

Sheena just smiled and checked her list. 'I think that covers everything.

'What about colour of eyes?' I said unkindly.

'We can't be too fussy,' she said. 'After all, it won't cost us anything. Just a donation to the funds.'

We drove over that afternoon. The girl in the office had a pleasant smile. She looked at Sheena's list and nodded. 'No problem,' she said briskly. In my experience this is always an ominous phrase.

We followed her out to the kennels, each in its own wire-enclosed run. 'I'll show you what we've got,' the girl said. 'Then you can choose.'

There were half-a-dozen mongrels. Large, shaggy, dog-type animals with understandably anxious expressions, thin legs and frayed tails. They looked like illustrations in an anti-vivisectionist pamphlet.

'You've no pedigree dogs, I suppose?' I said.

She looked at me reproachfully, as a shop-steward might look at a racist Personnel Officer. 'We have two, actually,' she said.

The first was Chan, a portly, middle-aged chow-chow in a slightly moth-eaten fur coat. He regarded us speculatively, his eyes as coldly calculating as the shrewder thoughts of Chairman Mao.

'No,' Sheena murmured in my ear.

I agreed. I could imagine Chan relaxing with a pipe in a Shanghai opium den but not living in our kitchen. Not after George who had been known to get high on half an aspirin.

'We really wanted a bitch,' I said defensively.

'Oh?' the girl said. 'Well, there's Alice. She's a real lady.' She rattled the gate of the next run and clicked her tongue encouragingly. After a minute or two, Alice emerged from her kennel, moving slowly and with great caution. She was a black greyhound with a very white muzzle and a formidable weight problem. She tottered towards us, wheezing and gasping, pausing frequently to lean against the wire mesh. At the gate she lay down (collapsed, more accurately), put her head on her forepaws and wearily closed her eyes.

We looked at her in astonishment. It isn't every day you come across a fat greyhound. Then I said, for something to say, 'How old is she?'

Alice opened her eyes briefly and looked up at me without affection, clearly offended by so indelicate a question.

'We're not absolutely sure,' the girl said. 'About six, I think.'

My own estimate was nearer sixteen.

'She's never been raced, of course,' the girl said, like a dealer on a car lot trying to off-load a second-hand MGB roadster.

I nodded. That I could believe.

'Isn't she ducky?' the girl said. 'And such a sweet temperament.'

But old and obese and in need of an Eventide Home, preferably with a trained nursing staff and a good dietician. As the companion of a lively young boy she was a non-starter.

We thanked the girl for her trouble, genuinely moved by her devotion to her abandoned charges, a little appalled by the thanklessness of her task. She put me in mind of a Salvation Army lassie ministering to the victims of some canine Skid Row. The pound note we slipped into the box on the office counter was pure conscience money. And she knew it.

Driving home, we stopped to buy the local paper. Alsatians, Great Danes, Old English Sheepdogs—they were all there in the PETS FOR SALE columns. Aristocratic giants, Kennel Club registered, inoculated, with pedigrees going back to William the Conqueror. All you needed was your own oil well and you could take your pick.

And then we saw it. At the foot of the page, like a light at the end of a tunnel. 'WANTED. Good homes for dogs and cats.' And a telephone number.

When we got in, I rang up straightaway.

'So, here is Smith,' a woman's voice announced peremptorily. A thick, rasping voice, Teutonic as sauerkraut. 'Vot you vontink?'

I had a mental picture of iron-grey hair, tailored skirt and jacket, sensible shoes, a pincenez. Daunting. I said, 'It's about this advert in the paper. We're looking for a dog and...'

'Vot kind?' she said, cutting me short. I gave her a quick run through the list.

'Is goot. Your name unt number?'

I told her. Humbly.

'Ja. It vill take perhaps forty-eight hours. Is understood?'

'Yes. Thank...' But she had hung up.

I slept indifferently that night, visited by bizarre dreams of dachshunds wearing rimless spectacles and Tyrolean hats, and was wakened at seven by the phone.

'Ve have for you der bitch,' Frau Smith said without preamble. 'Is younk. First cross Keeshond. Dutch, ja? You vontink?'

'It's not too large?' I said, trying to imagine what a Keeshond looked like. Crossed with what? I wondered.

'Is small.' She gave me a telephone number. 'Is Mrs Pemberton. You rink.'

Having taken the precaution of eating breakfast first, I rang Mrs Pemberton. She had the sort of voice you hear in those expensive little dress shops in Tunbridge Wells;

carrying, condescending, excruciatingly refained.

'Delaighted,' she said. 'A sweet little creature. We've quaite lost our hearts to you, haven't we, Pippa dolling?'

Pippa growled. Quite a deep growl, Dutch as Edam cheese.

'She's not a big dog?' I said warily.

'Nor ever will be. She's the daintiest of eaters, aren't you, my poppet?'

Pippa growled again. Hungrily.

'A teeny little appetite, haven't you, precious?'

Her trick of including the dog in the conversation was beginning to make me nervous. 'Perhaps we could come over and see her later this morning?'

'Delaighted,' she said. 'What fun, dolling. You're going to meet your new Uncle.'

I didn't much like the sound of this but, as Sheena said, we were adopting the dog, not her foster owner.

'Foster mother, by the sound of it,' I said darkly.

It turned out to be a substantial house in Surrey, all fitted carpets and expensive reproduction furniture and Sanderson wallpaper. Mrs Pemberton matched the decor as tastefully as a blue Persian cat on a silk cushion. She was dressed with the elegant simplicity of the very rich. A woman, I decided, who had everything. And knew it.

We stood by the window in the enormous sitting-room, sipping sherry and looking out over half an acre of lawn.

'She's a little shy with strangers,' Mrs Pemberton said, 'so Ai've put her in the garden.' She smiled archly. 'She's a very outdoor girl, y'know. Ah, there she is now, bless her.' She pointed to a laurel bush.

I saw a pointed face with large bat ears and huge pale eyes watching us covertly.

Mrs Pemberton opened the window. 'Pippa. Come along, dolling. Mummy's here.'

The bat ears swivelled, the long pointed nose tested the air suspiciously. 'Come and meet your Aunt and Uncle, then,' Mrs Pemberton cooed.

The dog shot out from behind the bush, streaked across the lawn towards us and disappeared round the side of the house. She was light brown, with the long, bushy tail of a fox. And she could certainly move. She flashed back into view, circled the lawn setting up a new lap record and skidded in behind the laurel to stand panting with only her head visible.

'Isn't she lovely?' Mrs Pemberton said fondly.

'She's a beaut and no error,' Sheena said in her best Earl's Court accent.

It was aptly said. Pippa's tail was fox, but her head, with those bat ears and pale, wild eyes was pure dingo.

'But a shade too large for us, I'm afraid,' I said diplomatically. 'She needs a lot more space than we can offer.' Like New South Wales.

Mrs Pemberton smiled understandingly and with some relief. Having heard Sheena do her Crocodile Dundee bit, she obviously considered us to be unsuitable relatives for Pippa.

I got through to Mrs Smith again after lunch. She seemed undismayed. 'Is too large, ja?'

I said a spaniel was more what we had in mind. Preferably a cocker.

'Cockers is difficult. All peoples vant. But ve try.'

In the next three days she sent us to see a spoiled and irritable Peke, a Corgi which specialized in nipping ankles, and a Dalmatian without spots. Her enthusiasm was undeniable as was her resourcefulness. Less impressive was her ability to grasp our wishes. Perhaps if I had been able to speak German it would have helped. But I can't. And with less than a week to Drew's birthday there was no time to take a crash course.

Then, with three days to go, Mrs Smith cracked it.

'Der cocker I have founded.' Abrupt as ever over the phone, her voice was mellowed now with a hint of triumph. 'Is small. Is clean. Is a bitch. Is goot, ja?'

'Wonderful,' I said and took down the address.

In the car, Sheena said, 'Now let's not build on it too much.'

'No way.'

'She'll probably turn out to be psychologically disturbed, with ear canker and a thing about small boys.'

'Probably.'

'I mean, if all peoples want a cocker, why hasn't she been snapped up?'

'Why indeed?'

More modest than the Pemberton residence (a good omen?), the house was a chalet bungalow in a quiet suburban avenue. Quiet, that is, until I rang the bell. The response was shattering. It was as if I had switched on a tape recording of the sound track of *Call of the Wild*. Above a groundswell of deep, hoarse barks, high-pitched yelps rose in an ecstatic descant. The door itself shook under the impact of leaping bodies. Passers-by looked round, startled.

From inside the house a woman's voice shouted, 'One moment.'

Sheena looked at me, eyebrows raised.

The woman called, 'I'm going to open the door now. Please come in quickly.'

She did. We did.

The hall was small and dark and alive with dogs. We stood knee-deep in a tide of leaping shadows, waving tails and lolling tongues. Talking was impossible. We focused on the face of the woman, a pale oval in the gloom, and smiled bravely. She pushed open the living-room door and we waded in after her. The dogs flowed round us, panting now but mercifully silent. 'Please sit down,' she said, 'before they grab all the seats.'

Sheena and I sat on a small settee, flanked (on her side) by a limp-eared approximate Alsatian whose mother had probably been young and certainly foolish. And (on my side) a very old, very correct Kerry Blue. The woman, Mrs Fletcher, sitting on the carpet with dogs piled up all round her, pulled the Alsatian down off the settee with an apology. But the Kerry Blue was allowed to stay. He sat at attention, looking to his front, the hair above his bright old eyes cut in a short, thick fringe like a misplaced Old Bill moustache. His name was Hero and he alone, of all the dogs there, belonged in the house. The others were temporary guests awaiting new owners. He reminded me of a Chelsea Pensioner whose favourite pub had been invaded by a disco.

Mrs Fletcher pushed a wisp of hair off her forehead and smiled the guarded smile of an experienced social worker faced with a couple of do-gooders. She was in her early forties, pleasant, without frills. She was also extremely skilled in eliciting information without actually asking for it.

In the course of five or six minutes of apparently casual chat she discovered the size of our garden, the fact that our house was centrally heated and the kitchen free from draughts, Drew's age and character and the bonus point that I worked from home so that the house was rarely empty. 'You've had a dog before?' she said.

We told her about George.

She nodded. 'We don't get many bulldogs. So now you want a cocker?'

'For Drew,' I said. 'She'll be his dog.'

'With a little help from us,' Sheena said.

Mrs Fletcher stood up, shedding two Jack Russells, a rather superior King Charles spaniel and the front half of the Alsatian. Her smile dropped its guard. 'You'll do,' she said. 'I'll get Jane.'

Sheena said, 'Jane?'

'The black cocker.'

She went out of the room. We sat with fingers crossed. Beside me, old Hero cleared his throat—a dry, my-glass-is-empty sound. I fought an impulse to ask him what he would have.

Then Mrs Fletcher was back with Jane under one arm and we were on our feet, all doubts dismissed, all hopes fulfilled. Jane was small, black and quick of eye and tail. Her coat shone, her teeth gleamed, her tongue was healthily pink.

'Oh, yes,' Sheena said. 'Please.'

We took Jane home with us, fully kitted-out with basket, blanket, brush and comb, collar, lead and pedigree. There was nothing to pay.

'All these,' Mrs Fletcher said, waving a hand over the assembled canine company, 'come from broken homes, one way or another. Our job is to find permanent homes for them. A dog is for life, you know, and needs commitment on your part. If you want to send a donation to the Society, that's entirely up to you. There's no obligation at all. I'm satisfied Jane will be loved. That's all that matters.'

I nodded. All you need is love. And commitment for better, for worse, in sickness and in health, till death... There were, I thought stroking Jane's black velvet muzzle, many worse recipes for a happy life—for dogs and people. But none better.

Mrs Fletcher waited for Sheena to get into the car and then put Jane on her lap. 'Any problems, give me a ring,' she said.

But there have been no problems. Jane has accepted us—all of us—with quiet approval which becomes, when Drew arrives home from school, ecstatic and frenzied adoration. She is gentle, intelligent, affectionate and (as Drew says happily) 'Altogether beautiful.'

I rang Frau Smith in the evening of his birthday to thank her for all her help. Her comment was a succinct summary of our own feelings.

'All is goot,' she said, 'if endink is vell. Ja?'

'Ja,' I said. And meant it.

166

LET THERE BE HEROES

I met him at one of those charity cheese and wine affairs designed to sweeten the sorrow of parting with money. He was a restless, intense young man, thin as winter sleet and as unforgiving. Behind rimless glasses his eyes were accusing in a face untouched by laughter. Prosecutor's eyes with the prosecutor's tunnel vision. A man who saw only what he wanted to see and who wanted to see only the worst. His name was Trevor.

He was holding a book. I recognized the portrait on its jacket as the latest victim of one of our literary hatchet-men.

'I suppose he's a hero to you,' Trevor said unpleasantly.

I smiled. 'Yes, as a matter of fact, he is.'

'Fact?' he said. 'Do me a favour. The fact is the man was a charlatan. Egotistical, arrogant, obsessed with his own imagined superiority.'

It was not a bad description of Trevor himself. I said, 'If you mean he didn't suffer fools gladly, I agree. With his responsibilities he couldn't afford to.'

Trevor's eyes narrowed. 'You know, of course, that he had a massive drink problem?'

'Fond of his food, too,' I said lightly.

He raised self-righteous eyebrows. 'It doesn't worry you?'

'No,' I said. 'Why should it?'

'Not by itself, perhaps. But taken in conjunction with his private life...' He shook his head. 'What a mess that was.'

'So I'm told,' I said, 'by those who don't respect other people's privacy.'

Trevor glared at me. 'People have a right to know about these things surely?' He patted the book smugly. 'It's all in here, fully researched and well documented.'

'I'm sure it is.'

'You should read it.'

'No thanks,' I said.

'Oh, that's so typical. You'd rather cherish your illusions than face the truth about your hero.'

I shrugged, 'Nobody's perfect.'

He blinked. 'You don't still admire the man?' he said, genuinely surprised.

'Very much. Don't you?'

'I'm not into heroes,' he said stiffly.

Except with a knife, I thought. 'No?'

'Heroes are for kids and peasants,' he said. 'It's time you grew up.'

But I was brought up on stories of the classical Greek heroes, men full of doubts and questions, flawed by weaknesses, far from perfect, who nevertheless glimpsed a vision of splendour and rose magnificently to the occasion.

It was difficult to explain this to Trevor. He and his muck-raking friends have the curiously childish notion that to command respect and admiration heroes and heroines must be perfect. No peccadillos, no character blemishes, no skeletons in the cupboard. It is an impossible demand and the disparagers know it. They make it their business to ferret out what they self-righteously call 'the truth', ignoring the achievements, concentrating ghoulishly on the faults.

So Captain Scott is presented as being an incompetent and peevish adventurer. Churchill as an unscrupulous opportunist and Florence Nightingale as a prim, frustrated spinster. Even if this were true it would not matter. The whole point about heroes is that they are human, as prone to error as the rest of us, yet able to perform extraordinary feats, overcoming their imperfections as a brave man overcomes his fear. What they are is unimportant. It is what they do that counts.

'Whatever his failings—and I'm sure he had many,' I said, 'his achievements stand out and cannot be denied. No smear campaign can diminish those.'

Trevor's smile was brittle. 'You're really into this hero-worship bit, aren't you?'

I shrugged. 'We all need someone to look up to. Someone whose life's work vindicates our own hopes and dreams. If such heroes did not exist we'd have to invent them.'

'Oh, we have,' Trevor said.

And indeed fictional heroes do stalk across our television screens and lie in wait for us on the shelves of the public libraries. Amoral, hollow creatures who embody not dreams but nightmares. They are hard-eyed and brutal, killing without remorse, coupling without love, rejecting the basic human values of decency, tolerance and forgiveness. Yet these shoddy half-men are skilfully presented as being praiseworthy models of courage and power; heroes to be admired and emulated. It is an appalling comment on our society that our children are being systematically robbed of their rich heritage in the achievements of great men and dedicated women to be given in their place Bonnie and Clyde, Dirty Harry, the detestable James Bond and a seemingly endless procession of serial killers. Characters devoid of virtue and compassion, strangers to honour, slaves to vice. Instead of creativity, destruction; instead of love, eroticism; instead of wisdom, cynicism. Stones for bread indeed.

On the far side of the room Trevor was busily shredding the reputation of a public figure with all the fervour of an old-style evangelist. I'm sure he saw himself as a fearless champion of the truth but he was peddling old gossip. Ancient history, in fact.

Debunking heroes is very old hat. Even Nebuchadnezzar's statue had feet of clay, Gladstone's concern for the women of the streets was salaciously misinterpreted, Canute's shrewd little parable of the incoming tide depicted as the misplaced pride of a foolish old man. No wonder Oliver Cromwell insisted on being painted pimples, warts and all.

Now there was a man who understood human frailty. A tragic hero in the classic mould, he knew that while we may seem to discredit an imperfect hero we would certainly destroy a perfect one.

'I can find no fault in this man,' Pontius Pilate said. But he had him put to death just the same.

A BOUQUET OF BRIDES

As the taxi slowed for the turn, a girl came out of the corner shop, saw me, smiled and waved vigorously. A pretty girl in her early twenties, young enough to be my daughter.

'Nice,' the driver said, clicking his tongue. 'Makes you wish you were young again.'

'You speak for yourself,' I said, 'I'm marrying her on Saturday.'

He raised astonished eyebrows, not knowing that I have been marrying pretty girls, usually on a Saturday, for the past forty years...

Time has blurred their faces and stolen their names. But some I still remember well. Like Dora.

There was something special about Dora; a quality of enthusiasm as infectious as laughter and as warming. Delectable in full-skirted white dress, train and veil, she sailed up the aisle on her father's arm. Her smile embraced the congregation. As she passed each pew the rows of faces lit up like a series of fluorescent tubes. All brides are said to be radiant. Dora certainly was.

We floated through the service on a tide of delight. The groom made his declaration of love—a slightly husky, 'I will'—and I turned to Dora. She smiled encouragingly, listened to the haunting question which begins: 'Wilt thou have this man...', tilted her chin and said in a clear, confident voice, 'You bet.'

I sometimes have misgivings about a wedding. But not about that one.

The wedding day belongs to the bride, of course. She is the focus of attention. The star outshining all others. Even with the expert aid of Moss Bros, the groom cannot match her splendour and is over-shadowed in her presence. In taking his name she takes also his glory. But there are exceptions.

When old Hans Marais, black of face, grey of hair, asked me to conduct his daughter's wedding in my church I was happy to agree. The Marais family were Cape Coloureds and my congregation was exclusively white. But liberal and understanding.

'She's marrying a Coloured man, is she?' I said, just to make sure. This was in Pretoria in the Fifties when the South African laws refused to accept inter-marriage across the colour bar.

'Ja,' Hans said. 'From Jo'burg. He's a good boy, Reverend.'

And Sophy was a nice girl, the colour of milk chocolate, with black curly hair and enormous dark eyes.

'Fine,' I said. 'When?'

'Soon, Reverend. I'll let you know the date.'

Unfortunately he forgot to do that, having many things on my mind, not least the cost of the reception. So when he knocked on my door ten days later and said, 'We are all here, Reverend,' it was something of a surprise. Especially as I was having lunch at the time.

I slipped across the garden to the vestry, put on my cassock and went into the church. There was a large congregation, all Coloureds, ranging from Zulu black through light brown to ivory, the women in bold floral dresses, the man in dark suits and cheap white cotton gloves.

Sophy and her bridegroom were waiting for me, flanked by the best man and old Hans. She smiled at me shyly, clutching a bunch of brilliant tropical flowers. I smiled back. Sophy I knew, the groom I didn't. He was black and slim and handsome, his skin African, his hair and eyes Chinese. A striking combination which gave him great presence.

I realized with some dismay that I didn't even know his name—something else Hans had forgotten to tell me. I leaned forward and said quietly, 'I'm sorry. What is your name?'

'Wonky John,' he said with enormous dignity.

I swallowed. Africa is a country of unusual names but this was ridiculous. I looked at Sophy. She smiled and nodded. I looked at old Hans whose dark eyes met mine serenely. 'Wonky John? ' I said incredulously.

They all nodded gravely.

I detected a flicker of anger in the groom's eyes. A man's name is important to him and not to be quibbled about. But—Wonky John?

I can't do it, I thought, looking miserably at the congregation which was growing restless. I can't go through the whole service saying things like, 'Wonky John, wilt thou have this woman...?' And 'forasmuch as Wonky John and Sophy have consented...'

But I did, expecting at any minute that the whole congregation would collapse in laughter. The Coloured have a marvellously irreverent sense of humour. Not surprising, considering that they are trapped between two cultures, disowned by both. But all went smoothly and with grace.

In the vestry afterwards I asked to see the registrar's certificate, relieved to find that Hans had at least remembered to bring that. I looked at it, signed the Marriage lines and gave a copy to Sophy. 'For you, Mrs Wong Kee Chong,' I said carefully.

The bridegroom shook my hand.

I also treasure the memory of the bridegroom in my Surrey church who arrived carrying a brown paper parcel, much at odds with his immaculate morning dress, which contained a pair of brand new, straight-out-of-the-box shoes. He changed into them in the vestry beforehand (and thriftily changed back again afterwards), in order (as he said) to show the congregation a clean pair of soles and heels when he knelt with his bride to pray. I've forgotten his name, but it wasn't MacTavish.

Then there was the tongue-tied, blushing young couple in a hurry who wanted to get married quickly by special licence because, as the girl said, 'We're going to have a caravan.'

They had grabbed it, fully-furnished, before someone else could step in, thereby saving a great deal of money. A valid reason for getting married in haste. But not the one I was expecting.

Weddings, like life itself, are occasions of beauty and purpose shot through with human comedy. This is as it should be. We are imperfect creatures, vulnerable to mishap, clumsy when we should be deft, hiding our shortcomings under elaborate ritual and carefully treasured little superstitions. And laughter is the forgiveness which rescues us from disaster. As was discovered by the bride's father at the Cana wedding in Galilee, who listened with relief as his guests laughed delightedly, enjoying the wine made by the Carpenter of Nazareth to extricate him from an embarrassing situation...

The taxi driver, still slightly shaken, dropped me at the station. I paid him and smiled. 'In my job,' I said wickedly, 'pretty girls are always asking me to marry them.' He looked at me with a kind of envy. 'Any vacancies?' he said hopefully.

A LOVESOME THING?

There are very few disadvantages in being British, but one is that people assume you are enthusiastic about gardening. About gardens too, of course, but that is not a problem. I am as content in a garden as Adam was in apple-blossom time with a glass of lemonade in one hand and Eve perched prettily on his knee. To sit in a comfortable chair on the lawn on a summer's afternoon surrounded by a blaze of herbaceous borders, listening with equal delight to the song of a blackbird and the muted, distant horns of cars stuck in a traffic jam on the road to the coast—this is bliss indeed. But the unremitting drudgery of all that lies behind it—the digging, the mulching, the raking, the hoeing—is the serpent in Eden.

In France and Italy, where they leave gardening to the professionals, this attitude is understood and respected. Not so in Britain. Here, the man who dislikes gardening is regarded with deep suspicion as being one who has a major character flaw. I wonder why? Nobody objects to people who like listening to music but have never learned to play an instrument, so what's so special about gardening?

I am earnestly informed by my neighbours (keen amateur gardeners to a man, woman and pre-teenage child but otherwise sane and worthy citizens) that gardening is pleasantly therapeutic. I have not found it to be so. Nor, I suspect, have they. Watching them straightening aching backs after an hour's weeding, teasing rose thorns out of their fingers after pruning and wheezing over a clay-clogged spade between April showers, I reflect that one man's therapy is another man's slipped disc, septicaemia and possible coronary.

Nor is the suffering all physical. There is also mental scarring. Amateur gardeners are prone to the chronic melancholia of the continually disappointed, the result of putting their trust in the impossibly magnificent pictures on the seed packets.

I well remember my own sense of outrage when the giant sunflower seeds, so carefully sown to mask a boundary fence, turned out to be rather stunted marigolds. Such a disillusioning experience, repeated with variations year after year, breeds incurable discontent. Which, presumably, is why gardeners, like their big brothers, farmers, are so difficult to please. If you politely decline to walk round their plots admiring the rockery, the daisy-free lawn and the ubiquitous gnome fishing futilely in the plastic-lined pond, they are peeved and careful to show it. If, on the other hand, you take the grand tour, enthusing over everything from berberis to beetroot, they invariably shake their heads and say, 'Ah, but you should've been here last week when the gladioli were at their best.'

Originally a garden was a place in which to grow food for the family. In many parts of the world it still is. When an

African villager sends his wife into the garden it is to plant mealies not magnolias. I can see the merit in this (although my wife is less convinced) and have even tried it myself. It was not a success. Whatever we planted, nothing came up but lettuces. No beans, potatoes, sprouts or celery. Just a vast green carpet of lettuce. And we don't even like lettuce. Which is just as well because the slugs ate the lot.

For people in the business of creation, gardeners are astonishingly destructive. A great deal of their time and money goes on killing things off. Nettles, thistles, docks, slugs, caterpillars, flies both black and green—all fall victim to gardeners' ruthless determination not so much to commune with nature as to rearrange its balance. The garden, looked at objectively, is a place of primitive passions where the birds kill the snails, the cats kill the birds and gentle, kindly matrons in gloves and wellies commit mass murder with chemical spray guns.

I shall never forget the cultured, considerate man, my host for the weekend, who hurried me out of the station into his car because he was anxious to try out his flame-thrower (a birthday present from his equally charming wife) on a particularly tenacious patch of weeds before the light faded. Which is why I was immensely encouraged last summer to read an article pleading with us to let a bed of nettles grow naturally in our gardens because so many insects need them. A humane practice I have been following for years.

This whole business of weeds is ethically dubious. I write as one who is never absolutely sure until they flower (and not always then) which are weeds and which are respectable suburban plants. Why is a dandelion a valued wild flower when growing in a hedgerow along a country road, but a tiresome weed on the lawn? And if, as I suspect, weeds are flowers the way God made them, who are we to tinker with his handiwork? If you know of a better excuse for not weeding, I shall be glad to hear it.

FULL CIRCLE

From all of which you may conclude in a fit of righteous indignation that we live in a house completely surrounded (and half-hidden) by rampant meadow grass, cow parsley, nettles and an army of insects. And undoubtedly you would be right. Were it not for George.

George is a retired professional gardener of the old school. The sort of flower-growing, lawn-taming man of the soil Kipling wrote about. Small and muscular, calm of eye, at peace with himself and the world, he is as different from the amateur gardener as an English oak from a bonsai tree. He gives us three hours of his skill every other week throughout the spring and summer. In that time he cuts three lawns, weeds all the flower beds, ties up what needs to be tied up, prunes what needs to be pruned, drinks two large mugs of very sweet tea and works miracles.

Some men have a way with horses; possess within themselves a natural authority which communicates itself to animals with a softly spoken word, an almost casual gesture. George is like that with a garden. Until he arrives it crouches behind the fence, a shaggy, snarling tiger turned man eater. As soon as he comes through the gate, pushing his ancient bicycle, it quietens and is stilled. Weeds come out at the touch of his hand, soil turns effortlessly on the blade of his spade, grass surrenders to his measured tread behind the mower. It is all smooth and unhurried, performed with that easy grace which is the hallmark of the professional. He scorns gloves, kneelers and chemicals and is the despair of the local Garden Centre with its shelves of expensive pesticides. Nettles don't sting him, the sun doesn't scorch him, the flowers obviously adore him.

From my chair under the apple tree I watch (but do not covet) my neighbour's wife hacking and wrenching and poisoning with the fervour of a priestess cleansing a defiled piece of holy ground. I shake my head sadly (she is really a very intelligent woman) and turn with relief to contemplate George's leisurely ministrations, intrigued at how slowly he appears to work, how quickly he accomplishes his tasks.

'That's looking better now, sir,' he says, scraping the spade clean before putting it away.

It is a magnificent understatement. The garden purrs in the sunlight, a tiger turned pussy cat. I look at this man with awed respect. 'How d'you do it, George?'

He smiles, as perhaps the Lord God smiled at Adam when they walked together in the garden in the cool of the evening. A slow, warm smile, infinitely reassuring, touched with mystery. ''Tis just a knack, like, sir,' he says modestly.

But it is more than that. Like Adam in Eden, I know genius when I see it.

TERMS OF REFERENCE

I was halfway through the *Times* crossword, doing rather better than usual, when Sheena looked up from the magazine she was reading, 'Why do I always use Glop?'

'I didn't know you did.'

'I don't, actually.'

'Very sensible,' I said worrying away at 9 across, a nine letter anagram of ferocious complexity. 'It sounds revolting.'

'But if I did?' (my wife can be persistent) 'Why would I?'

'Why would you what?'

'Use Glop,' she said patiently. A shade too patiently.

'I'm sorry, love. I don't even know what Glop is.'

'You put it in the washing machine to soften the water,' she said as to a slightly backward child.

'There's your answer, then,' I said and cracked 9 across. Now, 6 down...

She shook her head. 'Everyone's going to say that.'

I put my pen down carefully (only cowards use a pencil to do the crossword). 'Could we perhaps start again?'

'If I'm not disturbing you?' she said sweetly.

'Not at all.'

'Oh, good. It's this competition, you see. You have to solve three clues and then write a short, pithy sentence beginning: "I always use Glop because..." '

'What are the clues?' I said.

'Oh, I've done those. They're easy. All I need is half-a-dozen words for the slogan.' She looked at me in a way I have always found impossible to resist.

I resisted it. 'You'll think of something,' I said gallantly and picked up my pen. 6 down was obviously a pun on...

'The first prize is a new car,' she said quietly.

'We've got a car,' I said with less than my customary grace. There may be men who can do the *Times* crossword while carrying on a pleasant conversation with their wives. I am not one of them.

'This one is a BMW convertible,' she said.

I felt a flicker of interest. 'It is?'

'Special edition. Finished in the colour of your choice.'

'That,' I said, 'is different.'

She nodded. 'I thought perhaps it might be.'

Three mugs of black coffee later, I ripped yet another sheet of paper off the pad, crumpled it and dropped it on to the small pile of rejects on the floor beside my chair.

'No good?' Sheena said.

'Useless. It's such a ridiculous name. Glop. What rhymes with that except slop?'

'Hop, top, shop?'

'Much too obvious.'

'Vox pop? ' she said, And wickedly, 'Trollop?'

'See what I mean?'

'The slogan doesn't have to rhyme, of course.'

'Beanz meanz,' I said darkly,

'Oh yes, I see.' She put her hand on mine. 'I've been thinking.'

'So have I,' I said bitterly, 'for all the good it's done.'

'No, listen. Why not ask Mike?'

It was a brilliant suggestion. Sneaky, but inspired. Mike is an old friend of ours, reliable, always ready to help. More to the point, he is the senior copywriter in a reputable advertising agency.

I dialled his number. 'Mike, I want to pick your brains,' I said and explained about the competition.

'Ah,' he said with professional crispness. 'What's the infrastructure on this?'

'The what?'

'Terms of reference. Who's it aimed at? Up-market career girl living in a Chelsea pad? Or harassed mother of three in an end-of-terrace off the Mile End Road?'

'It makes a difference?' I said. A question so foolish he ignored it.

'Then there are the people who live in a soft water area. Devon, Lancashire, South West Scotland. How d'you get them hooked on a water softening agent? And what about the medical angle? People with allergies or sensitive skins. Can they trust the product not to aggravate them? And that's just for starters. You want more?'

'No thanks,' I said, feeling like Pandora five minutes after she had opened the box. 'It is a bit complicated, isn't it?'

He chuckled, 'What d'you think I get paid for? Slogans don't grow on trees. You have to work at them. Without the proper terms of reference I wouldn't know where to begin.'

'No. But somebody's got to win that car,' I said doggedly.

'Oh, right. Out of twenty thousand entries for this competition, one's going to hit the jackpot.'

'Long odds, eh?'
'Too long for me, I'm afraid.'

I should have been depressed by this conversation. In fact, I was comforted. If the artificial world of advertising is built on carefully researched terms of reference, why not the real world?

Like most people I worry about violence in the streets, cruelty to children, drug abuse, the erosion of family life. Dramatically highlighted by the media (for whom good news is no news), these things paint a disturbing picture of life as being a vicious game of chance offering glittering prizes for the lucky few and misery for the rest of us. A selective, grossly distorted picture in which ordinary people are portrayed as hapless victims of blind fate.

The truth is much more reassuring. Most children are born into the security of a stable, loving family. For every mindless vandal terrorizing the innocent there are thousands of decent citizens with time and sympathy to spare for their neighbours—witness the hugely generous response to an appeal from any good cause. The traditional values upon which our public life is based may be stridently mocked by trendy minorities, but most of us still recognize their worth. Honesty, tolerance, integrity, kindliness—these are still the true terms of reference which provide us with a pattern which endures; a recipe for happiness and hope. Life is not a game to be played ruthlessly at the expense of others but a skill to be learned and enjoyed. And taught to our children. Faith, hope and love—these still abide and cannot be denied.

No, we didn't win the BMW (or indeed any of the consolation prizes). Only fair, I suppose, since we still don't use Glop. In any event, the ultimate driving machine (whatever that means) is not really our image. As Sheena cheerfully admits, we are more the small-family-saloon-middle-aged-and-beginning-to-limp-a-little-on-the-hills type.

Thank God there are still a lot of us about.

A CERTAIN STYLE

The father of the bride wore a grey morning suit and topper hired for the occasion. He had a flower in his coat and a diamond stick-pin in his carefully tied cravat. No expense spared and everything a perfect fit. He should have looked impressive but he didn't. There was something missing; an elusive, indefinable quality no tailor can provide. Inner confidence, perhaps, a natural grace. Style.

In spite of the old song, style is not something you can put on. Either you have it or you don't. Watching him posing with his daughter for the photographer, I thought of a man who did. The late Lord Ballantrae.

I met him one afternoon at the gates of my church in downtown Auckland. He was then Sir Bernard Ferguson, Governor General of New Zealand. He got out of his car, tall, ramrod straight, enormously impressive in a dark lounge suit of impeccable cut and a black bowler hat; unmistakably military, completely at ease. His aide made the introductions and we shook hands, his eyes smiling down as he towered above me on the pavement. He turned towards the church.

Leaning casually against the railings, hands in pockets, ancient trilbies pushed back, two no-hopers grinned at him, small men in shabby suits worn with open-necked shirts, thin, home-rolled cigarettes in their mouths, eyes slitted against the smoke.

One of them nodded cheekily. 'G'day, sport. How're yer goin'?'

Sir Bernard stopped in mid-stride, screwed his monocle into his eye and looked them up and down. I winced, waiting for the crunch. He smiled, raised his hat courteously, gave them a half-bow and said, 'I'm very well, thank you. It's extraordinarily good of you to ask. How are you?'

It was superbly done and completely sincere, without a hint of condescension. Three short sentences which made them his equals. They straightened, hands out of pockets, dog-ends out of mouths. 'Right as a bank, sir, thanks.'

Sir Bernard gave them a brilliant smile. 'Splendid.' As we walked on through the churchyard, he said to me, 'Great chaps these Kiwis, Padre. Rough diamonds, some of them, but the quality's there.'

Later, after the service, we gathered in the church hall for coffee. It was a special occasion involving the University. The dons lined up in their academic robes and he shook hands with each one, greeting them with genuine pleasure as if they were old friends, as if the privilege was his, not theirs.

One of the women serving coffee was Jean. In her youth she had been a missionary teacher in Samoa when Sir Bernard's father (then Governor General himself) had made an official visit to the island. I told him this and said she would like very much to meet him. 'Of course,' he said. 'My pleasure.'

I introduced her and made a tactful withdrawal. From across the room I saw them in deep conversation, Sir Bernard laughing, Jean's face flushed with excitement. She was elderly and unassuming and he made her feel, as he had made the no-hopers feel, suddenly important and cherished. She made a little, slightly unsteady curtsey when they had finished talking and he bowed and kissed her hand.

And that's style.

It is not, of course, a male prerogative. When that same Jean was in her early twenties, way back before the war, she had visited Britain on a working holiday, speaking about her work as a missionary in churches up and down the land. In between, she spent time discovering the places she had heard and read so much about as a girl growing up in New Zealand; Canterbury Cathedral, Stonehenge, Fountains Abbey, St Paul's, Hadrian's Wall. For a young woman away from the Pacific for the first time in her life it was a marvellous experience. But not without its problems.

She was on a very tight budget and travelling light. A warm coat, one good dress, a couple of tweed skirts, three or four jumpers—you know the kind of thing. She managed very well with this limited wardrobe (nobody expects missionary teachers to be fashion models) until one weekend when she was invited to an important church on the south coast. On the Saturday afternoon she spoke of her work in Samoa. She wore her favourite skirt and jumper and made an excellent impression; a slim, pretty girl, modest and smiling, in love with her job, her enthusiasm infectious. Within five minutes she had her audience spellbound, describing a world none of them had ever seen. There were no package holidays to New Zealand and the islands then.

Afterwards she was whisked away by her host and hostess to spend the night in their home. She was a little taken aback by their large, chauffeur-driven car and positively stunned by their house. It was one of those country mansions standing in several acres of parkland, the great gates guarded by a lodge. Not at all the sort of place she was used to staying in. Her nervousness increased when the door was opened by a butler who addressed her hostess as: 'My Lady'.

In the spacious hall, my Lady said, 'I expect you'd like to rest a little before dinner, dear. We've invited a few friends in to meet you.'

A maid took Jean's bag and took her up to her room. When she had gone, Jean opened her suitcase, thankful that she had brought her one good dress. But when she opened the case and took the dress out—disaster. Somehow the top had come off the bottle of shoe-cleaning liquid packed in the case. A long brown trickle oozed wetly down the bodice and across the skirt. Even if it would wash out (which she doubted) the dress would never be dry in time to wear to dinner that evening.

Jean sat down on the bed and wept.

An hour later she heard a gong sound in the hall below. She smoothed down her tweed skirt, checked her hair in the mirror, tilted her chin bravely and went out on to the landing.

Going down the magnificent staircase she heard the subdued murmur of voices, a little burst of laughter. She saw the butler hovering near the foot of the stairs, fought down an impulse to turn and run back into her bedroom and slowly descended, giving him a tentative smile. He looked at her in disbelief. 'Madam will be dining?' he said.

'Yes,' Jean said firmly.

The butler swallowed, opened the door of the drawing-room and ushered her in.

The large, spacious room was full of people standing about with glasses in their hands, laughing and talking. They were all in full evening dress; the men in dinner jackets and black ties, the women in long, expensive gowns and high-fashion shoes, the lights glittering on bracelets and earrings. Jean stood just inside the door, her legs trembling, her face very pale. The impulse to run was suddenly very strong but she couldn't move.

'Ah, there you are, my dear. Come and be introduced.' Her hostess held out her hands in smiling invitation. She was poised and beautiful in a gorgeous silk dress which must have cost more than Jean earned in a year. But her eyes were gentle.

Jean crossed the room, acutely aware of amused (and in some cases disdainful) glances from the guests as they took in her jumper and skirt and those brown, sensible, low-heeled shoes.

She heard a woman drawl, 'My dear, nobody warned me it was to be a fancy dress affair. Who do you suppose she is? The little goose girl?' and felt her face flush hotly.

Her hostess gave her a glass of sherry and introduced her to a polite, very distinguished looking couple before slipping discreetly away with a murmured apology.

Jean sipped the unfamiliar drink and felt sick. The elegant couple were making pleasant conversation but she wasn't listening. She was looking at the dresses of the other women, remembering that stained, crumpled horror in her bedroom and imagining everyone was talking about her, laughing at her behind their hands.

'... very different from Samoa, I expect?' the distinguished looking man said.

Jean made an effort, 'Aw, yis,' she said, her New Zealand accent unusually broad, 'Too trew ut us.' And wished the floor would open up and swallow her.

It seemed like an eternity before the door opened again and her hostess reappeared. When she did, the room suddenly went very quiet. Every head turned to look at her. She was no longer wearing that marvellous dinner gown, the satin, high-heeled shoes, the necklace of diamonds and rubies. Instead she was in a jumper and skirt worn with brown walking shoes.

She crossed the room serenely, put her hand on Jean's arm in a warm gesture of welcome and said, 'Finish your sherry, my dear, and we'll go in to dinner.'

And that's style. With a capital S. Or, put another way, loving your neighbour.

THE GIFT OF SPEECH

I n the beginning was the Word; the gift of speech.

Cows happily chewing the cud in a sunlit field may well be thinking deep, philosophical thoughts, dreaming dreams alive with beauty; but they can't talk about them. Only people can do that. Cows ruminate, people communicate. Words are the basic tool of human society. If communication breaks down, nothing gets done. The author of the ancient myth of the Tower of Babel understood this. Cursed with a multiplicity of languages, the builders of the tower were unable to complete it, divided by the one human gift which should have united them. A tragedy echoed in any meeting of the United Nations Security Council

But it's not just a matter of different languages...

Invited to speak at a Literary Society dinner in a Southern Irish city, I was met at the airport by the Vice-President. He was small and wiry with the black hair and bright, reflective eyes of the true Celt and his welcome was as warm as his smile. I took to him at once.

Driving me into the city he said, 'Did you get a meal at all on the aeroplane?'

I said I had finished an excellent three-course lunch only minutes before landing.

'Ah well, never mind,' he said in his lilting, peat-smoke voice, 'you'll be having your dinner early, so you will.'

I was still wrestling with the logic of this when we arrived at the hotel. He took a briefcase off the back seat of the car and we went inside. A splendidly impressive woman, regal in a black velvet dress with lace at her throat and wrists, was sitting at a table just inside the conference suite. After we had been introduced (she was the Secretary), she said, 'Did you manage to get rid of all the brochures, Michael?'

The Vice President opened his briefcase and produced a handful of leaflets. 'Ivery last one of them,' he said proudly, 'and here's what's left over.'

I looked at him, bemused, suspecting a joke. But she nodded. 'You're a darlin' man, so you are,' she said, gracious as a queen conferring a knighthood.

The Irish may have a special genius for separating words from their recognized meaning. But they don't hold the monopoly.

Matthew and Dorothy were in their sixties and wearing well. A comfortable devoted couple, he gentle-eyed and kindly, she fiercely protective of him. He was a Methodist minister with a circuit of small village chapels strung out across Exmoor. We stayed at the same hotel that summer and found them to be pleasant company.

When we enthused about their life in the peaceful

countryside, Dorothy's mouth tightened. 'All right now in the good weather,' she said, 'but not when winter comes. I don't like him turning out on a dark, wet night to drive over those country roads. Not at his age.'

Matthew smiled apologetically. 'We're not on the phone, you see.'

'It would make such a difference,' Dorothy said wistfully. 'He could just pick up the phone in the warmth of his study and keep in touch with people that way.'

'I've asked THE POWERS THAT BE,' Matthew said (he was the sort of man who puts such phrases into block capitals), 'but they tell me the funds won't run to it. Not at the moment, anyway.'

'Not ever,' Dorothy's voice was tart, 'as long as you keep mollycoddling them with visits when a phone call would do.'

I said, 'Is there a public phone box nearby?'

'Oh yes,' he said. 'Just across the road from our house.'

I said I supposed he could use that sometimes, although it wasn't as convenient as having a phone in the house, of course.

'It's not that,' Dorothy said. 'We could put up with the inconvenience but it wouldn't solve the problem.'

'No?' I said.

Matthew shook his head. 'You see, most of our church people aren't on the phone either.'

If there was an answer to that I didn't know it. And still don't.

In a different category, but no less traumatic, is Richard.

Richard is a judge's clerk, a man of experience and learning well-versed in the law, trained to choose his words with care. And yet...

When I rang him recently to suggest lunch the following week he said regretfully that he would be in the Midlands from Monday. His judge was going out on circuit and where his judge goes, Richard has to follow. So it was with some surprise that I ran into him the following Wednesday on the District Line platform at Victoria in the height of the rush hour.

'Aren't you supposed to be in Birmingham?' I said.

'Yes,' he said, a touch peevishly, 'but we're running late with the list. Still at the Old Bailey.'

We boarded the tube train and stood jammed together just inside the doors.

'It's this murder we're doing,' Richard said. He's a big man, heavily-built, with a clear, carrying, court-room voice.

A shudder of apprehension rippled down the carriage. Startled eyes appeared over the tops of newspapers. The people standing next to us tried to push further down the aisle.

'It's taking longer than we anticipated,' Richard said solemnly. 'You never know with murders. Complicated things.'

The newspapers quivered. A woman sitting in the nearest seat gripped her handbag with white-knuckled hands and stared wide-eyed at Richard. In his expensive black overcoat, pin-striped trousers and highly-polished shoes he didn't look like a murderer. But how does a murderer look?

'A killing in cold blood,' Richard said earnestly. 'It takes some sorting out, y'know. Not something to be rushed.'

'No,' I said. 'I suppose not.'

'Even when you've done as many as we have,' he said, 'you still run into unexpected snags.'

'I'm sure,' I said, wondering when someone was going to pull the communication cord and hand us over to the police.

'And the worst of it is,' Richard said gloomily, 'when we've done this one we have to go to Birmingham and do two more. Rather unpleasant ones, as a matter of fact.'

196

THE GIFT OF SPEECH

I got out at the next station. Not surprisingly, so did everyone else in that carriage—except Richard. Through the window I watched him sit down and pick up a paper, totally unaware of the sensation he had caused.

But it's not always so amusing. The divorce court, the estranged daughter living in a squalid squat, the victim of racial intolerance afraid to answer a knock on his front door—all evidence of the breakdown of communication. None of them is funny. Yet each is a microcosm of the barrier of words people build against each other. A comical misunderstanding in a crowded train becomes the match to light the fuse of violence in a housing estate, a political crisis across a disputed frontier, a night of terror in an African township, the tears of children in the ward of a hospital devoid of food and medicine and hope.

There is little point in possessing the techniques needed to bounce our words off a satellite if what we are saying makes no sense to those who listen—or, worse still, the wrong kind of sense. We have the technology to build a splendid tower of human achievement and happiness. But have we the necessary understanding, the forgiveness, the grace?

In the beginning was the Word and the Word was with God and the Word was God. Perhaps the key to all our longing, all our fears, is to start taking that statement seriously.

COMING THROUGH THE RYE

I was twelve at the time and innocent, as small boys were
back in the early Thirties when a shilling a week was
big pocket money and a holiday on the Isle of Bute was
a great adventure.

My Scottish grandfather saw to that, filling every day
with new excitement. Six-foot-two in his hand-knitted
socks, blue of eye, black of hair and wickedly handsome still
at sixty, he was a true romantic, chivalrous as a John
Buchan hero, with a head filled with dreams and an eye for
a pretty woman. My grandmother (who was tiny and
smiling and whom he adored) fed me enormous meals of
porridge and eggs (breakfast), Ayrshire beef and roast
potatoes (lunch) and Loch Fyne kippers, floury soda scones
and wedges of solid fruit cake (high tea). For his part, my
grandfather nourished my imagination with brave stories of

Bruce and Wallace and the gallant, doomed Chevalier whose heirs, he confidently believed, would one day regain the throne. And with the lilting poetry of Robert Burns.

It was to Burns's cottage in Alloway we went that day, as pilgrims to a shrine, taking the morning paddle-steamer out of Rothesay to Wemyss Bay. I remember the dazzle of sunlight on the water, the white tower of Toward Point lighthouse, the wooden deck trembling beneath my feet to the thrash of the great paddle-wheels. And the woman standing alone in the prow, her silk headscarf fluttering in the wind. She seemed quite old to me but was probably no more than thirty-eight, slim and poised in tweed coat and skirt, leaning forward over the rail as if to urge the boat onwards. There was something about her—a kind of eagerness, a sense of expectation—which intrigued me.

It intrigued my grandfather too, stimulating his fertile imagination, 'Bonnie Mary of Argyll,' he said with a wink, 'awa' tae meet her lover.'

'How d'you know that?' I said, not altogether sure what he meant by lover. It was not a word twelve-year-olds were au fait with in those less sophisticated days.

He smiled mysteriously. 'When ye get a wee bit older, laddie, ye'll ken how, so you will.'

As if aware that she was being talked about, the woman turned her head, looking back down the length of the deck. Framed in the head-scarf, her face was pink from the sea-breeze; a pleasant, open face with a determined little chin and eyes the colour of violets wide-set under level brows. I was still impervious to feminine beauty (all the ecstasy and heartaches still to come) but those eyes fascinated me. There was candour in them and an astonishing serenity. And something else—a melting, vulnerable look I did not understand.

But my grandfather did. 'Bedroom eyes,' he said, raising his hat with his customary gallantry.

The woman gave him a quick, warm smile and turned back to the rail.

My grandfather sighed. 'Aye, laddie. Yon's a heartbreaker if ever I saw one.'

But I didn't understand that either. Not then.

At Wemyss we hired a car with a driver. My grandfather steadfastly refused to learn to drive, being of the firm opinion that it was not a suitable pursuit for a gentleman (always excepting Sir Malcolm Campbell of whom he thoroughly approved). This did not, however, deter him from giving a great deal of gratuitous (and dangerously misleading) advice to the man behind the wheel. Perhaps because he was called O'Leary. My grandfather had little time for the Irish, considering them to be Lowland Scots who had squandered their birthright and been banished like remittance men across the sea.

O'Leary certainly looked the part. He wore an ancient leather flying coat and a shapeless green hat which combined with his wizened face and sharp, coal-black eyes to give him a distinctly fey appearance. It was as if we were being driven, with reckless disregard for the Highway Code, by a slightly manic leprechaun.

Fortunately, there was little traffic outside the towns, the road following the coast through Largs, by Irvine and Prestwick, to Ayr. An ever-changing panorama of white sand beaches, green hills fluffy with sheep, the purple peaks of Arran, the wide sea beckoning us down to Ailsa Craig and away towards Ireland. My grandfather was in his element, peopling the peaceful landscape with ghostly heroes who had fought to defend their farms and families against the marauding Vikings. As I listened to him, the centuries rolled back and I could picture the longships rounding the Mull of Kintyre, stealing up through the morning mist to ground in the little bays, their helmeted crews storming ashore to pillage and burn. The rattles which infested the car became the clatter of swords on shields. The flash of sunlight reflected in a cottage window blazed like a torch tossed on to the thatch to fire the village. Every mile was a page turned in a chronicle of valour, every page redolent with courage and glory. Even O'Leary was impressed, gripping the wheel with small, dirty hands, nodding his head in appreciation. 'Sure and it's a brave tongue ye have in your head, sorr,' he said, winking at me in the mirror.

We did not linger in Ayr. A cheesy town, my grandfather called it, curling his lip in distaste. I stared at the drab, grey buildings, the clutter of trucks in the narrow streets and knew what he meant. This was no longer the sleepy little market town Burns had known and loved. Ten minutes later we came to Alloway.

We stopped just outside the village. My grandfather gave O'Leary half-a-crown for his lunch and told him to meet us again at four o'clock sharp. We watched him turn the car and head back towards Ayr for beer and sandwiches and maybe a dram to settle it all down. Then we began to walk up the street, soaking up the atmosphere; a small boy trotting beside a long-striding man with a blackthorn stick in his hand and a picnic basket tucked under his arm, treading softly on a poet's dreams.

The village drowsed in the midday sun, bright with flowers, little changed (apart from the paved road) since Burns had lived there. I sensed magic in the warm air, would not have been surprised to see Tam o' Shanter and his crony Soutar Johnnie come reeling out of the inn, clamber up on to their horses and gallop away with the Devil at their heels. It was that kind of a place, that kind of a day.

The cottage we had come to see stood long and low under its thatch by the roadside, looking much as it must have looked two hundred years before. Except for the car parked outside it; an open MG sports car, conspicuously red, gratingly modern. My grandfather gave it a long, outraged stare, turned his back on it firmly and ushered me into the house. It was all there as he had promised. The bed in the wall, the quill pens set out on the writing table, the portraits on the walls immortalizing the memory of the young smuggler turned exciseman who had put the soft lilt of Lowland Scots into the annals of literature. There were the glass-cased manuscripts yellowed with age, the ink faded, the writing bold and angular; the simple handmade furniture solid on the stone floor, the array of iron cooking utensils hanging above the empty hearth.

And there, come upon suddenly in a doorway between two rooms, was the woman with the violet eyes on the arm of a fair-haired, soldierly man in a British warm, cavalry twill trousers and highly-polished brown shoes.

They stood aside politely to let us pass, the woman smiling in recognition. It was cold in the cottage, little sunlight finding its way through the tiny windows, but her smile touched me like a warm hand. I felt myself blushing awkwardly, as if it were her house and we uninvited guests. As they moved into the room behind us, my grandfather shook his head enviously. 'Some men ha'e all the luck,' he said. 'And him an Englishman, forbye. Ye've only tae look at him tae see that.'

'Perhaps she's not Mary of Argyll after all,' I said. 'She could be bonnie Lesley, gone over the border to spread her conquests further. Like Alexander.'

He gave me a quick grin, recognizing the quotation, unable to disagree with Burns in his own house. 'Aye, mebbe so, laddie.'

'Like my mother did,' I said.

He frowned fiercely. It was a sore point with him that my mother had gone south to find a husband, compounding the insult by giving birth to me in an English city. It was not that he disliked my father, just that he thought of him as being a foreigner. 'Och, weel,' he said and sighed. 'Naebody's perfect.'

The red MG was gone when we came out. My grandfather was pleased about that. We made our way through the village and into the woods, found a grassy bank by the little river and sat down to eat our picnic; morning rolls stuffed with ham and cheese, drop-scones thickly buttered, a large blackcurrant pie oozing juice, two apples, a bottle of beer for him, lemonade for me. 'Just a wee bite tae put ye on,' my grandmother had said, packing the basket that morning as we finished our porridge and started on a platter of fried eggs and bacon with toast and marmalade to come. 'There'll be a proper meal waiting when ye get back.'

After we had eaten, my grandfather settled his back comfortably against a tree and lit his pipe. 'It's places like this gi'ed Rabbie his inspiration, laddie. Bonnie braes and bonnie lassies were aye food and drink tae him, so they were.' He took his hat off, as if in church, and began to sing. 'Green Grow the Rashes', he sang and, 'For A' That An' A' That' and the queen of them all, 'My Love Is Like A Red, Red Rose', his voice deep and gentle with the chuckle of the river behind it. I listened with tears of pleasure in my eyes, emotionally stirred by something beyond my comprehension, which is the magic of poetry.

We rested for a while and then set off again, following the river, whistling 'The Road To The Isles'. And came out of the trees and climbed the bank to a narrow path and heard the sweet, clear sound of a violin. I remembered that Burns himself had played the fiddle (we'd seen it hanging on the wall in the cottage) and shivered with sudden excitement mixed with awe. In that timeless, haunted glen nothing was impossible.

But the fiddler, when we saw him, was not a young, bold-eyed poet with a smile to break a girl's heart. He was an old, old man sitting in a wheelchair with a tartan rug over his knees, the violin tucked under his chin, his fingers gnarled and bony on the strings. And yet there was a feyness about him, an other-worldly quality which made the hair rise on the back of my neck. A finch was perched comfortably on his hat and another on the tip of his bow. Sparrows sat in a row along the parapet of the old stone bridge and a magpie strutted arrogantly in front of him, cocking its bright-eyed head, charmed by the music. He was playing 'The Flowers of the Forest', the pure notes falling like tears in the sunlight, the murmur of the river under the bridge a sigh for brave men killed in battle.

He finished the piece, spoke softly to the birds and nodded to us. I wanted to clap but felt it would be out of place after so poignant a tune. 'Shall we give him something?' I said.

My grandfather shook his head. 'He's no' playing for money, laddie. Only for his ain pleasure.'

The fiddler adjusted his bow, the finch flying up to join the one on his hat. He closed an eye in a slow knowing wink and began to play again; a jaunty, sly little tune I recognized immediately.

Gin a body meet a body
Comin' through the rye
Gin a body kiss a body,
Need a body cry... ?

I looked across the bridge and saw them come out of the wood together, arm-in-arm and smiling, the Englishman and the woman with the violet eyes. My grandfather chuckled and I knew why. He had told me that the song was not about a girl walking through a field of rye. Rye was the Scots word for a ford—stepping-stones across which a girl would walk with her skirts raised above her knees, to the delight of the watching young men. I smiled uncertainly. As I said, I was only twelve at the time.

The couple stopped in a patch of sunlight at the far end of the bridge. The woman was still smiling but her eyes were unusually bright.

'She's crying,' I said, surprised. 'Why is she crying?'

'Because she's in love wi' yon Englishman and he wi' her,' my grandfather said. 'And it's no' right, ye ken. No' right at a'. And that's the pity o' it, so it is.'

We left them there with the fiddler and the birds and the quick, saucy music, tactfully withdrawing under the trees to make our way back to the village. O'Leary was waiting in the car. It smelled like a brewery.

'Are ye sober, mon?' my grandfather said accusingly.

O'Leary looked hurt. 'Sure and would Oi be otherwise, sorr, wi' yersel' and the boy in me care?'

My grandfather grunted and wound down the window, helpfully issuing instructions on the finer points of making a three point turn. We had only gone about half a mile when I heard the blare of a horn and the red MG flashed past us with a throaty snarl of exhaust, the Englishman driving, the woman beside him.

'Will ye look at the feller go,' O'Leary said admiringly as the MG took the next corner in a controlled drift and disappeared. 'We'll no see him again this day.'

'Except in the cemetery,' my grandfather snorted. 'Mad Englishman.'

But we did.

We took a different route through Ayr, avoiding the busy town centre. It brought us past the railway station. The MG was parked at the kerb, the couple standing on the pavement locked in each other's arms, oblivious of the people round them. She was standing on tip-toes and he was kissing her—very thoroughly.

'Ae fond kiss and then we sever,' my grandfather murmured, half-wistful, half-disapproving. And then, to me, 'Dinna gawp, laddie. It's no' polite.'

But I had already forgotten them in the excitement of O'Leary's driving.

Until we walked down the jetty at Wemyss Bay to board the steamer and saw her already on deck, one gloved hand on the rail, her face pale and set, a still, lonely figure, all her morning eagerness drained away.

'Has her soldier left her?' I said, surprised.

'Aye, mebbe,' my grandfather said. 'Or she's left him, more like.'

'What's the difference?'

He sighed. 'There'll come a day when ye'll ken that, laddie.'

The sun was dropping down the sky, Arran's Sleeping Warrior etched black against the gold, the wind chilly now off the water. We went straight down into the saloon for tea; scones with strawberry jam, pikelets, chocolate eclairs. Moments later she was there, smiling down at us.

'May I join you, gentlemen?' Her voice was a pleasing contralto, the accent not so broad as my grandfather's but unmistakably Scots.

He stood up and pulled out a chair for her and she sat down composedly and ordered tea. She took off her headscarf and shook her hair loose; honey-coloured hair with a curl in it and that firm little chin, those wide-set, violet eyes. My grandfather squared his shoulders, eyeing her appreciatively.

'Did you enjoy your day out?' she said, smiling at me.

'Thank you, yes,' I said shyly. And, remembering my manners, 'Did you?'

She laughed. 'Very much.'

'Aye,' my grandfather said meaningfully. 'We noticed.'

She looked at him levelly. 'Things are not always what they seem.'

'No.' His eyes went to her wedding ring. 'Mebbe not, Mrs...?'

'No names,' she said quickly. 'It's sometimes easier to talk to a stranger.'

'Or no' to talk at a',' my grandfather said.

She shook her head. 'I need to talk to someone.'

He looked at her shrewdly but not unkindly. The way he looked at me when I was in trouble. 'Aye,' he said, 'I think ye do.'

I began to lose interest in this adult conversation. The fresh air had made me drowsy. The saloon was warm, the muffled beat of the engines soporific, my stomach comfortably full. Their voices faded as my eyelids drooped and closed. When I opened them again, the woman was saying, '... posted to India with his regiment. We'd only known each other three weeks when he sailed. Three wonderful weeks but...' she smiled wryly. 'We wrote to each other, of course, for a year or two. But increasingly I felt I was writing to a stranger. Someone I might never see again. It was different for him. He had his life out there— excitement, the company of his fellow officers, polo, leave in the mountains. But all I had was a memory.' She shook her head. 'And then I met James. He's a good man Understanding, kind, loving in his own gentle way. He made me feel—wanted. Secure. He was here, you see, and Peter wasn't. When James asked me to marry him I said yes.' Her smile was radiant. 'I've never regretted it. Not for one moment.'

'And ye're happy together?' my grandfather said.

'Oh yes. Fifteen years married and as happy now as when he put the ring on my finger. It's just that sometimes I...'

I must have nodded off again then, because the next thing I remember she was saying, '... touch and go for a time and then he began to recover. The doctors said it was a miracle and I suppose it was. But it's left him a cripple. He'll never walk again.' She tilted her chin bravely, 'He's marvellous about it, my Jamie. Never complains. Always so cheerful. But sometimes it breaks my heart to see him sitting there so helpless.' There was a catch in her voice, the glitter of tears in her eyes.

My grandfather put his hand on hers across the table. 'I'm sorry, lassie. Verra sorry.'

She found her handkerchief and dabbed at her eyes. 'And you—you don't think it was wrong of me to see Peter today? Just the once, for old times sake?'

'For auld lang syne,' my grandfather said, dreamily quoting his favourite poet. 'Ye chose the richt place tae meet. Rabbie was aye kind tae lovers.'

'We were never lovers,' she said quickly, colouring a little. 'It was all quite innocent and... I mean, we didn't...'

'Just a cup o' kindness, was it?'

'Something like that. Peter was my first love and when I stepped off the train this morning and saw him standing there I—well, I was a young girl again, just for a moment or two, and he...' She shook her head impatiently. 'You'll think me very foolish.'

'Not at a'. Just human like the rest of us,' my grandfather said gallantly. 'Is he married now himself?'

'Only to the regiment.' She smiled ruefully. 'He's not the marrying kind, I see that now.'

'They're aye the dangerous yins, ye ken,' my grandfather said in his best Presbyterian voice.

She nodded. 'It's all right, y'know. I'm not in love with him now. Not any more. I knew that in the first five minutes. That was partly why I went—to make sure. And partly because—well, I'm still fond of him, I suppose. As a friend. Can you understand that?'

My grandfather smiled. 'Aye, I can.'

'James has all my love. I wouldn't—couldn't do anything to hurt him.'

'Does he ken where ye've been today?'

'No, he thinks I've been up to Glasgow to see a girl I was at school with. It—it's the first time I've ever lied to him.' She choked over the words, ducking her head.

'Whist noo,' my grandfather said. 'Ye're a guid wife and a brave yin. And bonnie, forbye. Ye deserve a day tae yersel' tae lay a ghost, so ye do. And nae harm done tae anybody.'

'You're very kind,' she said softly.

'Och awa',' my grandfather said uncomfortably and changed the subject. 'Ha'e ye been on Bute long?'

'Six months. We came down here from Stirling after the accident when it was obvious James would never work again.'

'Ye made a guid choice.'

'Oh, yes. It's lovely, So peaceful and...' She hesitated, her eyes pleading. 'You'll forget what I've told you? Please? Only Bute's a small place and people talk...'

My grandfather sighed theatrically. 'My memory's no' what it was. I'm an auld mon, ye ken. And auld men forget a' too easily.' He gave her a roguish, sideways glance. 'Whereaboots in Glasgae did ye say ye'd been?'

Her smile was dazzling; the sort of smile Rabbie Burns would have swum the Clyde in winter to see. 'I knew I could trust you. Thank you for listening—and understanding. You've done me so much good, the two of you.' And to my embarrassed pleasure she leaned towards me and kissed me warmly on the cheek. 'Love be kind to you, wee man,' she whispered, stood up gracefully and was away up the stairs to the deck.

My grandfather blew his nose loudly and glared at me in mock jealousy. 'Yon kiss wasna' for ye, mind,' he said darkly. 'So dinna look sae fu' of yersel'. It was meant for me, so it was.'

'Aye,' I said in my best Scots accent, 'I ken that fine.' And was rewarded with a grin and another chocolate eclair.

The saloon was emptying now as we approached the Rothesay pier. We went up on deck to watch the mooring ropes expertly thrown and caught, the gangway lowered (these little maritime rituals are important to small boys). The woman with the violet eyes was first off the boat, hurrying across the pier to where a big-shouldered man with a thin, lined face and a thatch of white hair was waiting in a wheelchair. He looked strained and tired but his eyes lit up when he saw her and the kiss she gave him was long and fierce in a tender sort of way—very different from the one she had given me.

' "Gi'e me a canny hour at e'en, my arms about my dearie O," ' my grandfather quoted, nodding sagely. 'So that's what made her cry on the brig this afternoon.'

'What did?' I said, remembering, not understanding.

'Yon auld fiddler, laddie. He was in a wheelchair too, was he no'?' He shook his head. 'And here was me thinking she and that English soldier were...' And left the sentence prudently unfinished.

The Asgog bus was waiting at the pierhead and we got two seats at the front. Settling himself beside me, my grandfather said, as if to himself, ' "True it is, she had one failing; had a woman ever less?" ' He looked at me. 'The guid Lord kens we're none of us perfect, laddie. But loving is forgiving and that's his greatest gift tae us a', so it is.' He smiled, 'When the time comes, remember that and ye'll no gae far wrong.'

And when the time came, some ten years later, I remembered. And he was right.

As we rounded the point at Craigmore he put a cautionary hand on my shoulder. 'Mind, noo, laddie. No' a word tae your grandmither aboot yon lady. 'Tis her secret we're holding, so it is. Mak' sure it stays that way.'

And so it has for nearly sixty years. Until now.

A Traveller's Tale

'Oh, by the way,' my hostess for the weekend said on Sunday night, 'you'll find our Visitors' Book in your room. Be a dear and put something in it for us, will you?'

I smiled, masking my disappointment. I had, until that moment, thought her the ideal hostess. Relaxed and gracious with a cheerfully intelligent husband and a sure touch with the coq-au-vin, she had entertained me royally. But none of us is perfect.

'My pleasure,' I said untruthfully.

It was on the bedside table, a large, expensive affair bound in white calf. I eyed it balefully. I dislike Visitors' Books, partly because I write an execrable hand few people can decipher (and they only with difficulty), and partly because I can never think of anything to say. There are those who can conjure up an apt (if fawning) quotation at the drop of a bedroom slipper. I am not one of them. Sit me down at a well-laid dining-table in congenial company and I can quote the famous with enviable erudition. But alone in an unfamiliar bedroom at the end of the day my mind goes blank. This may be because I resent having to sing for my supper, however subtly I am invited to do so. A letter of thanks the day after my departure is much more my style— accompanied on very special occasions (as when there is no Visitors' Book) by a grateful tribute courtesy of Interflora.

I got ready for bed with a heavy heart and sat down with the book, turning the pages morosely, seeking inspiration. It is, after all, permissable to borrow someone else's quotation, provided a decent interval has elapsed between their visit and yours. Unfortunately, far too many previous guests had used this ploy (the habit of cribbing, once formed, is hard to break).

On page after pastel-tinted page, the same bons mots appeared, hackneyed as the mottoes in Christmas crackers. I found Burns urging his cup of kindness yet on friends and strangers; Isaac Watts discovering the virtues of good company and good conversation three centuries before Wogan; Stephen Grellet piously resolving to do the right thing because 'I shall not pass this way again'—a quotation much favoured by guests angling for a second invitation. All these ponderous old horses were well-placed. But leading the field, with more repeats than a James Bond movie on TV (and nearly as many as *The Sound of Music*) was R.L.Stevenson's dictum, invariably misquoted as: 'It is better to travel hopefully than to arrive'.

At first glance it is the perfect epigram, wise with a hint of cleverness. A pinch of instant philosophy guaranteed to leaven the lump of those serio-comic speeches people make at twenty-first birthday parties and wedding receptions. It has exactly the sort of up-and-away, life's-a-great-adventure ring to it which you would expect from the old romantic who gave us *Kidnapped* and *Treasure Island*. Such speeches, inserted between the champagne and the cake, are quickly made and as quickly forgotten. Which is just as well. For it is only upon reflection that the innate cynicism of Stevenson's words begins to emerge.

Here is an invitation to the journey of life; a brave call to embark upon a great expedition, travelling through the changing years towards a personal El Dorado of fulfilment at the end of the rainbow. It will not always be an easy journey. Nobody expects that. There will be shadowed valleys between the soaring, sunlit peaks, tears and failures as well as triumphs. But none of this will matter because the destination will always beckon, the rainbow curved with promise above our heads. And we will travel hopefully to find our dream come true.

Only—and here's the let-down—to discover, when at last we arrive, a monumental anti-climax. A shoddy reality miserably short of the shining dream which has kept us going through dark days and chilling nights.

And you can't get much more cynical than that.

I sat in that luxurious bedroom and thought about the guests who had slept there before me.

Why had so many of them chosen this particular quotation? To display their erudition, perhaps? Or, more honestly, because it summed up their own disillusionment? Is life no more than a cruel trick played on unsuspecting innocents, promising fulfilment only to betray our trust, giving us dreams of glory only to disappoint and mock us?

I remembered that other great romantic, Captain Scott. Sustained by the hope of a magnificent prize, he slogged through the endless blizzards, enduring the hunger and the bruising cold, only to find the prize already claimed by another when he finally reached his journey's end. That is how we see him; gallant, dogged, doomed. Is he, perhaps, the most representative of us all? Is that how history will see us?

My thoughtful hostess had provided some bedtime reading for me on the little table. A couple of condensed books viscous as condensed milk, an anthology of modern verse, Neville Cardus on cricket, Bunyan's *Pilgrim's Progress*.

Now there was a journey to stir the blood. The Slough of Despond, Doubting Castle, Vanity Fair, Mr Standfast, Apollyon, Christian. The dream of a tinker in a rat-infested cell, that has become a classic (which everyone admires and few ever read). I leafed through it, the pen and ink drawings like milestones on the journey, and came to that magic, climactic sentence: 'And so he passed over and all the trumpets sounded for him on the other side.'

So perhaps it is not, after all, an impossible dream. Perhaps we travel hopefully to an arrival of music and laughter, a destination of splendour beyond our wildest imagining. Only time will tell who was right; Stevenson or Bunyan. But I know which one gets my vote. 'In my Father's house are many mansions. I am going to prepare a place for you.'

What did I write in the Visitors' Book? The first words I hope to speak at my own journey's end. 'Thank you for having me.'

THE YEAR'S AT THE DOOR

If June is about roses, January is about doors.

The month is named for Janus, the two-faced Roman god who guarded the door of the year. The original janitor, in fact. Nobody believes in him now but every December, as the year turns, curious rituals are still observed in some families. Even Presbyterian ones. Especially Presbyterian ones.

When I was in my mid-teens I was appointed the priest of Janus in our predominantly Scottish family. My father was a redhead (and anyway English) and all my uncles on my mother's side were fair or bald or a bit of both. Janus would have none of them. He demanded a male with black hair. So it had to be me.

At five minutes to midnight on December 31, to the astonishment of our English neighbours, I was thrust out

into the night to stand shivering on the step, a lump of coal
in one hand, a small bag of salt in the other, and the door
firmly closed against me. Closed and locked and chained. It
was a moment of solemnity and high drama with just a
touch of fear. I remember the sighing of the wind through
the leafless trees, the cold, aloof brilliance of the stars, the
sense of being banished into primeval darkness with the
year dying around me and no guarantee that another
would be born. It was like standing on the precipice of
history waiting for the end of the world.

Then the church clock chimed the first stroke of midnight
and the spell was broken. I heard the rattle of the chain, the
grate of bolts being drawn, the turn of the key in the lock.
Ugly, wonderful sounds that were music in my ears. The
door was flung open. Light and warmth streamed out to
engulf me. Smiling faces, eyes bright with excitement,
hands outstretched in love to draw me back into life. Thrust
out to die with the year, I stepped back into the house
reborn.

The lump of coal went straight onto the fire, the bag of
salt on the white-clothed table. The wine was opened, the
glasses filled and raised up high.

'A guid New Year tae yin an' a',' I said lustily, the priest
reciting the versicle of hope.

'An' mony may ye see,' came the chorused response.

The toast was drunk, hands warmly shaken, kisses
exchanged. And my priestly duties were over for another
year.

It had its comic side, of course. The wine was always
ginger wine, drunk freely under the impression (mistaken)
that it was non-alcoholic. As a result, we all slept late on
New Year's morning and aspirins were in great demand.
And I inevitably caught a cold. But there was something
about the whole ridiculous performance I have never been

quite able to dismiss. An aura of mystery. A trauma of black despair routed by hope fulfilled.

I still remember the expression in the eyes of my aunts; exiled Highland women whose comfortable bodies housed minds steeped in the faery lore of their wild, native glens. And the respect in the voices of my uncles (Jacobites to a man) who, the following Sunday, would be model Presbyterians again booming their way through the metrical psalms, but who were, in those first, triumphant minutes of the New Year, at one with their Celtic forebears, enchantingly caught up in the mystery of time and eternity they called Hogmanay.

Perhaps it was all foolish nonsense, outmoded superstition as incongruous as a claymore in a nuclear age. And yet...

The word Hogmanay arrived in Scotland from France as hoginane. And hoginane itself was a corruption of the old French agiullanneuf—a gift at *l'an neuf*, the new year. A gift from Rome to ancient Gaul in the days when Janus really was a god to be revered.

Christmas is Christmas and Easter is Easter, historical events, not myths. Events I will treasure with gratitude and will defend until life's end. But I am haunted still by Hogmanay in this slick, cynical twentieth century culture to which my children are heirs. For the imagery of the rites of Janus the doorkeeper is accurate and perceptive. The closed door which opens from darkness to light; the piece of fossilized tree (once the Yule log, symbol of the ancient pagan god Yol) burning on the hearth to give warmth to the house; the salt which is the taste of life itself, clean, astringent, enhancing all its flavours. To stand outside in the dark with the salt and the coal; to go inside when the door opens and put the coal on the fire, releasing the power of the sun. This is Incarnation and Resurrection re-enacted in the winter cold. Life renewed in the gift of a new year.

Now we have central heating and there's no fire on the hearth on which to put the coal. We buy our salt in plastic containers and use it sparingly in food for fear of heart disease. The imagery of Janus, like that of Father Christmas, has faded and no longer captures the imagination of our children. None of us now makes that symbolic journey under the stars to the dark edge of time on New Year's Eve.

Instead, we watch the television party in Scotland, join a little self-consciously in the singing of 'Auld Lang Syne' with the kilted figures on the screen, drink a toast to the New Year (claret not ginger) and go warm to our beds.

Much more sensible, especially at our age. But something is missing—some magic, some mystery. A sense of awe.

The shadow of Janus stands lonely at the door of the year, a god without a feast, remembered only vaguely in the name of the month he heralds in. He never existed, of course. Just a mythical figure, the figment of some rich, if unscientific, imagination. But what of the truth within the myth? Is this no longer to be expressed, examined, believed?

On New Year's Eve I look out of the bedroom window at the stars and the shadows under the trees and think of One who stands at the door and knocks. One who came after Janus but was before him and will be long after the little god is finally forgotten. Not a mythical figure, he, but a living person, an integral part of our history and of our experience.

And I slip downstairs for a moment on some pretext about checking the locks and making sure the TV's unplugged, open the door and in silent gratitude let him in.

Also from Lion Publishing:

The 'Gift of...' Series
A striking blend of thoughtful writing and beautiful photographs makes each of these four books a gift to cherish.

The Gift of Friends
The experience of true friendship is one of life's most precious gifts—the enjoyment of shared interests and pleasures, deep understanding and communication, and mutual support in the crises of life...

ISBN 0 7459 3007 7

The Gift of Marriage
Insights into the attitudes that make for a deep and lasting marriage relationship. Moments of thoughtful reflection contrast with exuberant joy in this gentle and tender book.

ISBN 0 7459 3005 0

The Gift of a Child
The birth of a child is an occasion for rejoicing and celebration. This book captures the moods, feelings and dreams that accompany parenthood. And it explores the more difficult areas of discipline, responsibility and nurture—with hope and faith.

ISBN 0 7459 3004 2

The Gift of Years
This book will appeal to all who have reached or passed the middle years of life. It offers a gentle liberation from natural fears, celebrating the grand adventure of life in a spirit of hope and faith.

ISBN 0 7459 3006 9

The 'Celebrating...' Series
Beautifully illustrated collections of poetry, prayers and reflections to help you celebrate the milestones in life.

Celebrating Love
The many different dimensions of love are explored in this book, which puts into words the emotions we sometimes find hard to express. It makes an ideal gift for a partner or for those celebrating an engagement.

ISBN 0 7459 2397 6

Celebrating Marriage
Reflections on the special qualities and challenges of each stage of the marriage journey. It speaks both to couples just starting out together and to those celebrating a wedding anniversary.

ISBN 0 7459 2398 4

Celebrating Motherhood
Motherhood is a demanding business—whatever age your children are! But for most mothers it is also a deeply enriching experience, something they wouldn't change for the world. This book which celebrates all that it means to be a mother is an ideal thank-you gift for mothers of all ages.

ISBN 0 7459 2395 X

Celebrating Retirement
Retirement—a new beginning, a fresh start, time for yourself at last. But there are uncertainties too, and adjustments to be made. This book is a celebration of all the new possibilities that retirement offers.

ISBN 0 7459 2398 6